Praise for

Graduating into the Nineties

Every newly employed college graduate should have a copy of *Graduating into the Nineties*. Carter and June offer immediately useful information about the skills, plans, and attitudes that recent graduates need to succeed in today's competitive workplace.

—Barbara Hamilton, Ph.D.
Director, Freshman Rhetoric Program
Oakland University, Rochester, Michigan

Graduating into the Nineties is very perceptive. People who have worked for five years in the business world would learn from reading this book.

—Tony Ponturo
Vice President, Corporate Media & Sports Marketing
Anheuser-Busch, Inc.

Picture all college graduates reading and heeding Carter and June's advice . . . The success and satisfaction of new professionals would soar.

—Lynne Milburn
Director, Career Center, University of Texas at Austin

Graduating
into the Nineties

Graduating

into the Nineties

GETTING THE MOST OUT OF YOUR FIRST JOB AFTER COLLEGE

Carol Carter

and

Gary June

The Noonday Press

FARRAR, STRAUS AND GIROUX

NEW YORK

LIBRARY OF CONGRESS CATALOGING-IN-PUBLICATION DATA
Carter, Carol.
Graduating into the nineties : getting the most out of your first
job after college / Carol Carter and Gary June.—1st ed.
p.   cm.
1. Vocational guidance.   2. College graduates—Employment.
I. June, Gary.   II. Title.
HF5381.C367 1992 650.14—dc20 92-21945 CIP

Preface

The two of us began writing this book several years ago when Gary left Prentice Hall to take a job with a West Coast computer company. At that time, we had numerous discussions about the first few years out of college, life goals, and future opportunities. We decided to keep in touch by working together on a project which ultimately became this book.

We wrote *Graduating into the Nineties* because we learned the hard way how vastly work differs from school. When we first started working for Prentice Hall, we were green. We didn't have a clue as to what to expect. We learned a great deal in a short period of time—from handling a mediocre salary review to learning how to keep emotions in control during a heated work debate. We wanted to communicate what we had learned to those about to experience post-college life for themselves—from the trivial to the sublime. Looking back on our experiences, we wish some impartial person could have given us a few pointers; it would have soothed the growing pains.

As we began writing, we realized that our experiences in and of themselves did not encompass the working world. We had ideas, but we wanted empirical evidence. In addition, the working world of the nineties is different from that of the late eighties, when we started. So, with the help of Mary Vandeveire and Brian Sahd, we interviewed people at various career stages. We sought people from a variety of fields and companies—from retail sales to opera singing to accounting. Strangely enough, we heard the same chords resonate regardless of whom we talked to. We've tried to present those many chords as music in this book.

We have many people to thank for helping us make this book happen. Our special thanks to each and every person we interviewed. Your candor helped to illuminate the real challenges, and solutions, that are part of one's first job. Jean Godfrey-June, Gary's wife, read and commented on the entire manuscript and fielded endless phone messages and express packages. Brian Sahd and Leigh Talmage were our unofficial editors. Their comments and suggestions helped to define and sharpen the book from the earliest drafts.

Though we didn't tell our colleagues at Prentice Hall about this project (we thought it might jinx our ability to finish it), we sincerely appreciate their contributions to our health and happiness at work. Prentice Hall employs an incredible number of talented, capable, and entertaining people; it is a pleasure to be part of such a great company.

We would like to extend particular thanks to our editor, Elisabeth Dyssegaard, whose convictions and instincts often gave us the direction we needed. Her kind persistence kept us writing, rewriting, editing, and writing. Elisabeth has an integrity and commitment to her authors which remind us of the old days of publishing. We thank everyone at Farrar, Straus and Giroux who has helped to make this book a success.

A number of other people read this manuscript, and their comments helped make it a better book: Greg Ferro, Enid Lotstein, Gigi Veguilla, Amy Paterson, Pat Garisek, Leigh Talmage, Brian Sahd, Angela Quilala, and Corrine Stoewsand.

This book took us about three years to complete. In the middle of the process, we were each confronted with one of the most difficult experiences of our lives. In November of 1990, Gary's brother, Randy, died. A few months later, in early January, Carol's dad died of a heart attack. It is to Randall Loren June and John Henry Carter that we dedicate this book. They live on within us, inspiring us to do our best, to help others, and to be true to what we believe in. Their deaths have taught us more about living than any other experience.

Contents

Graduating

into the Nineties

The Snapshot:

Adjusting to Life and Work

Out of School

Education today, more than ever, must see clearly the dual objectives: education for living and educating for making a living.   *—James Wood*

I have never let my schooling interfere with my education.   *—Mark Twain*

There is more to life, Horatio, than is imagined in your philosophy.   *—Hamlet*

I will never forget that year. It was 1984. I was a senior in college at the University of Arizona. In less than eight months, I would be graduating, entering the unavoidable "real world." I was terrified. As a liberal arts major, I didn't know exactly what I was prepared to do. I knew that my education had taught me to write and communicate, but I wasn't sure how those "lessons learned" would translate into job-market skills. I spent most of the year actively worrying about what job I was going to get and how I was going to get it.

Early in the fall semester of my senior year, my brother Craig asked me: "What kind of job do you think you would like?"

"I really don't know," I responded.

"Well, what do you like to do?"

"I like to work with people. I like to plan and organize events. I like to help people."

"I bet you'd be a good manager," Craig said. "If you want ultimately to be a manager, one of the best places to begin is in sales."

"What do you have to do in sales?" I asked.

"I don't know," he said. "I've never been in sales. But I know it's one of the best places to start because it will help you build certain skills—such as working well with a broad variety of people and persuading people to see your point of view."

Even though my dad and mom had been in sales for years, I had never thought to ask them what it was they really did. I had almost no understanding of what it meant to be a good sales person. So I checked out some sales books from the library and started to research the sales jobs which were available through my campus placement office. I wrote to Procter & Gamble, Xerox, Hallmark, and almost every other company imaginable. One company that seemed especially interesting was Prentice Hall, publisher of college textbooks. For some reason, it was easier to see myself selling textbooks than any other product or service. It just felt right.

After a few months of interviewing, I was lucky enough to be offered a job by Prentice Hall. When I say lucky, I mean lucky. I had a few other job offers, but none I wanted as much as this one. That kind of match doesn't always happen, especially in your first job.

Signed, sealed, and delivered

I graduated from college on May 12. Two days later, on May 14, I was officially employed. It wasn't my dream location—Tempe, Arizona—but it was the only thing the company was offering at the time. Since I had lived my whole life in Arizona, I wanted to experience a different city. But it wasn't meant to be. At least, not then.

The first few days, weeks, and months on the job

I distinctly remember my first day. The sales representative I was replacing came over to my house to drop off all the files and the company car. We went over things briefly—the details of the paperwork, mainly—and that was it.

"Good luck," she said. "I hope you like the job." She had resigned to work for a competitor in California.

"Can I call you if I have questions?" I asked.

"Sure," she said. I knew I probably wouldn't call her. She wouldn't need another distraction while she was adjusting to a new job, a new city, and a new company.

I was petrified. A new job, a new city, no office environment to support me. I took the files, called my manager, who lived in another state, and asked her what I should do first.

"Spend a few days reading through your manuals," she said, "and then go on campus to meet secretaries, professors, and bookstore managers. Don't worry if you don't know exactly what to say and do. You'll learn as you go."

"I will?" I thought to myself.

From home study to the real thing

After a few days of reading about the job, I was supposedly ready to jump into the thick of it. My first day was a real experience. It was particularly odd because one of my accounts was on the same campus where I had gone to school. But now I was dressed in a suit, carrying a briefcase. I felt enormously self-conscious, especially when I saw some of my old friends who were on the five-year plan.

Since I was a "generalist," I sold textbooks in all areas. The fields I knew nothing about—electrical engineering, computer science, chemistry—seemed the most intriguing. But I began with my strengths. I went to the Humanities and Social Studies Departments first. I walked up the steps to the social science building and decided to call on some political-science professors.

"Professor Xing? I'm Carol Carter with Prentice Hall. Do you have a minute to talk?" (This was the first question suggested in the interviewing section of my Home-Study book.)

"Not right now," Professor Xing replied curtly.

"Okay. Thank you. Nice to meet you," I said, walking out with my tail between my legs.

A few weeks and many sales interviews later, I learned that I should have asked him for an appointment for later in the day. Thankfully, the other people I had planned to see did have time for me. Although I felt just as nervous, I gained confidence and learned more with each interview. Every two or three days I called my manager, Lisa, and told her what had happened.

"Does that sound normal to you?" I would ask.

"Relax, Carol. You are doing fine. But here are some things to think about over the next few weeks." She gave me a lot of good advice. I knew this wasn't typical. I spoke to some of my friends in other industries whose managers rarely spoke to them.

My first year on the job was filled with a number of comical and a few painful learning experiences. Gary also had some unusual experiences as a new graduate. Here is his story.

My senior year in college was extremely frustrating. Most of my friends were engineers and had no trouble lining up jobs well before Christmas. My other friends, liberal arts majors like me, either were heading off to graduate school or were taking time off. Unfortunately, I had neither the money nor the inclination to wait around until inspiration struck. I ended up trying a lot of things, interviewing for jobs, applying to the Naval Officer Candidate School and to law schools, before finally deciding to attend graduate school in Medieval English.

One month into graduate school, I realized I had made a mistake. I was enjoying the work and doing well, but there was a huge age gap between the other students and me. Both my roommates were over thirty, and I was a young twenty-one. I decided to leave after only one term.

I borrowed some money from my family, packed everything I had into my 1976 Dodge Dart, and drove to Denver, Colorado, to find a job. Because of all my tribulations and difficulties in deciding what to do with my life, I was very unsure of myself. I was also broke and in a new city. I knew only one person, my girlfriend (who would later become my wife), and she lived an hour away.

I found an apartment and started interviewing for every type of job imaginable. I had experience in sales because of jobs I'd had while I was growing up, so I looked there first. The Denver economy was poor, though, and I had to take what I could get.

I interviewed with everyone for everything: check printers, wine sellers, pipe fitters, restaurants, cash-register-machine makers, etc. I was so broke that I concentrated on just getting a job, so I wouldn't have to rely on my family. This was a big mistake.

I ended up with a job selling office equipment door-to-door in Albuquerque, New Mexico. After one week of training in Denver, where I basically memorized a script, I moved to New Mexico and started work.

The office was very small, only five people. They were friendly, but I was clearly the outsider. I had little direction and my job consisted, essentially, of driving to office complexes and making door-to-door "cold calls," sometimes as many as fifty a day. People did not want to talk to me, and business was bad. I grew to dislike my job intensely. I lasted a year, made little money, and acquired some sizable debts, before I reapplied to Prentice Hall, the last company I had interviewed with before taking the office-equipment job.

Looking back, I realize that I had made a mistake. I had underestimated myself and hadn't waited for the right job. Still, I learned some valuable lessons: how to handle difficult people, how to be consistent, and how to take charge of your personal life. Most important, I learned that knowing your own strengths and weaknesses is the first step to take to be happy.

That first inglorious struggle

Remember that everyone struggles during his or her first few years out of college. It's a big transition. Graduates respond to their jobs and their lives in different ways. For this book, we interviewed a lot of people—some recent grads, some not so recent. But everyone, when asked, remembers what it was like in those first years out of school.

Milton Medraza, after graduating, took a job as a security guard working nights at an apartment complex near a major state university. His biggest surprise? Some of the college students didn't respect him, because he looked young. After the security house was egged twice and the guard pole was run over, Milton requested a transfer to the daytime shift. It was much easier to deal with mail people and delivery personnel than with rambunctious college students. Two years later, Milt was promoted to night manager, and by then he was mature enough to deal with the difficulties.

Karen Xanthos, after graduating, got a job teaching math to sixth-graders. Her greatest adjustment? It was difficult to meet people her own age at work. All the other teachers were in their forties and fifties. She became good friends with Helen, an older woman who had a great track record as a teacher. Helen became her mentor. Still, she was much older than Karen, and their relationship was limited to work. Karen missed talking to people her own age. She felt lonely.

After a while, Karen realized that she needed to spend more time outside of work, meeting new people. Since she was in a new town, this was difficult at first, but little by little she developed a strong support network. How were the sixth-graders? Great. She discovered she liked them much more once she was able to separate her personal needs from her work. Because she was happier, she had more energy and vigor for her students—and their parents.

Tom Franklin's first post-college job was an extension of his college job. He had worked on the campus newspaper, and now he had a staff position at the local newspaper as a reporter. Tom was a good writer, but he had to get used to asking the tough questions that get to the heart of a story. Practice and persistence gave Tom the confidence he needed to ask probing questions and to get to the real story. He wrote some average stories before his better work appeared some years later.

Jenny Kilroy's first out-of-school job was as a nurse. She had had internships and plenty of patient contact, but her first week on the job involved a dose of real responsibility. As a pediatric nurse, she saw kids of all ages and with all kinds of illnesses. For the first time, she realized the impact she had on both patients and families. While learning the ins and outs of the ward and the staff, she learned a lot about herself and found strength within her that she had not known she had. Things like this—what the heart of the job is—you just don't learn in school.

Robert Rothman started as an accountant with a mid-sized firm after he graduated from college. His biggest adjustment was getting used to the seasonal nature of the work. During the summer, people in his office took four to five weeks vacation. Great, he thought, until tax season came and he understood why people at his firm got so much time off. During the month of April, Rob worked around the clock, including Saturdays and Sundays. Now he's used to it, but the first spring was like a solid season of final exams—week after week after week!

Points of reference

This book is about succeeding in your first job in spite of it all. To get the most out of this book, take it slow and answer the questions posed, on paper and in your head. Most important, strive for a greater understanding of who you are—your likes, dislikes, and strengths and weaknesses. Know thyself.

Beyond the Dorm

"Wait till you get to the real world."
"I wish I was back in school."
"You don't know how easy you have it."

After we graduated from college and started working, we discovered many similarities between our new world and our old: we had to plunge into work and give it the same kind of focus we did in our studies in school. We had to become comfortable learning entirely new skills. We had to be patient with our own learning curves, even though we wanted instant gratification. We had to meet new people, most of whom were different from ourselves, our friends, and the professors at school. We had to adjust to work lives as well as new lives off the job. It was hard to make new friends, get used to a new city, and keep up with personal chores such as cleaning the apartment and making car payments.

Making the adjustment

"When I got my first job, the biggest surprise was that someone was paying me to do a job that for six months I didn't fully understand how to do," says Amy Gonzales, who is a graphic designer for the Girl Scouts of America. "What I know now that I didn't know then is that this is completely normal. It took me a year before I felt really accomplished in my work and adjusted in my personal life."

Going from college to the work world is a lot like going from a bike with training wheels to a deluxe ten-speed. You are still the one behind the handlebars, but the vehicle—the core of your existence—is a lot more difficult to control. It may feel a little scary initially, but in the long run you have much more control. You decide where you want to go and the speed and quality of your ride.

Steadying the handlebars

You will make mistakes as you learn on the job. It is what you do with the mistakes that determines how well you will do in your career and in the scheme of life itself.

So, what exactly is it that you need to make a smooth and successful transition from college to the working world? First of all, you need help. That's what this book is for, to improve the odds. Second, you need the desire to grow, change, and incorporate new ideas and new habits into your life. Third, you'll need some courage, elbow grease, and persistence, because at times you will be tempted to give in to your own limitations or trick yourself into thinking that there is an easy way out.

You may not have realized it, but you have already opted not to take the easy way out. You have accomplished something worthy of admiration: you have acquired a degree. At at time when only fifty percent of Americans graduate from high school, let alone college, that is something to be proud about. Even if you didn't make the most of every opportunity along the way, you have nothing to be afraid of and every reason for optimism. You're on a roll!

In this book, we are going to keep you going by giving you the tools and knowledge you will need to be the victor in this endeavor. The question now is not: Will you flunk even though you have your degree? It is, rather: How far will you go?

How is college different from the "real world"?

Here is the good news and the bad news, not necessarily in that order.

1. *People depend on you.* For the most part, in college, if you miss class the consequences are not all that great. You see the professor to make up the material, do additional reading, get the information elsewhere. If you miss a test, you take it later or make up for it with other assignments.

At work, you can't do that. If you don't show up when people are expecting you, you may lose your job. Your peers and your manager may not be willing to fill you in if they think you should have been there. If you miss on a project or deadline, there usually isn't a chance to make it up. Everything and every day is a group project.

2. *You depend on others.* Don't try to do everything on your own. People depend on you, but you depend on them, too. You'll learn as much from your colleagues as you do from your manager or mentors.

3. *You make and meet deadlines.* The working world is much less structured than the college world. In college, people tell you when tests are to be given, when papers are due, when to register for classes, when to graduate. In the working world, sometimes people will tell you things and sometimes they won't. They will expect you to find out for yourself, set your own deadlines, and define the parameters of your job. In the beginning, you might feel naïve. That's fine. Ask questions—even if you feel awkward. Seek clarification of what you do not understand, and take the initiative.

4. *You learn to see shades of gray.* For the past few years, you've taken multiple-choice and true/false tests. You might have learned which chemicals combine to make a desired product, who did what and why

in the fifteenth century, how to use a computer, and all about man's inhumanity to man as seen in Shakespeare's *King Lear*. When you read your textbooks, go to class, and take periodic tests, it can seem as though what you are studying is all black-and-white. College is for the most part a series of discrete courses, without a lot of interconnections, outside of your major.

At work, however, there are a lot more shades of gray, because there is rarely one absolute right way of doing things. There are still good decisions and bad decisions, but what is good or bad isn't as obvious. A lot of times the answers you'll be choosing from are "All of the above" or "None of the above." We always hated those kinds of questions.

Some of the linear thinking, point A to point B, so common in college is useful in work. But the sooner you realize that there is more than one right answer and, more important, more than one way of getting at that answer, the more your mind will be at ease and the better you'll perform.

Sometimes it takes people a while to adjust to the ambiguity of business. Frequently, your job will be to figure out simply what the right course of action should be. This process, what people commonly call problem solving, is by definition uncertain. You take a problem and try to work through it, using whatever means you can. Making order out of this chaos may not be a large part of your first job out of school, but it will become increasingly important as you take on more responsibility at work.

CASE IN POINT
Gray but not too gray, by Rich Matteson

Rich Matteson, currently an MBA student at the University of North Carolina, told us the following story.

"During my last semester in college, I interviewed with about ten different companies. My degree was in hotel administration, with an emphasis in food and beverage marketing. I had two great internships under my belt, one with Macy's department stores in retail foods, and the other with Walt Disney World. The job offers I received were very diverse, from United Airlines to Houlihan's to large hotel chains. I ended up working for a hotel chain at a brand-new resort that was opening in Tucson, Arizona, my hometown.

"I was part of a four-person team responsible for the operation of the resort's specialty restaurant and nightclub. Opening in high season, we were instantly busy seven nights a week. I was the youngest of the managers and by far the least experienced in the restaurant business. During the first six months, a number of problems developed with the management team, ranging from drug use to blatant disregard for hotel policy.

"I was what I would call 'green,' and became so caught up in the daily operation of the restaurant that I began to sacrifice my own personal integrity. It became difficult to determine what was really right from what was really wrong. I had learned certain things in college but had trouble equating my past experience with the trouble I was facing now. The restaurant had a bumpy first year, but after some necessary management changes, it surpassed all expectations.

"I left this job after one year to pursue other interests. It was not until I had some distance from my former place of work that I realized how often I had sacrificed my personal integrity during that year. I know now that you can be taught many things in school, but you can't 'learn' to have integrity and common sense. Things may seem gray on the outside, but if you step back and take a look at what is really happening, it may be more black-and-white than you realize. You spend four or so years in college learning how things are supposed to be done, but you spend a lifetime developing your own instincts. If you sense something is not right, then it probably isn't. Don't be influenced by a smooth-talking superior who supposedly knows more than you do. No job is worth sacrificing your own self-respect. Always do the right thing."

---

5. *Your behavior counts.* In college, your professors teach a lot of students. They grade you on how well you know the material, not on how well you behave. In the work environment, you aren't just a name in a grade book (although you may occasionally feel that way!). You are the company. How you act, the clothes you wear, the way you deal with your co-workers, and the way you approach your work says a great deal about you and your long-term potential. And there will be a lot of people watching you. You may not realize it, but the higher-ups usually ask people you work with what you are like, what you contribute, how you deal with stress, how people like working with you, and how motivated you are.

6. *What you do takes longer.* One of the most difficult adjustments is the work schedule itself. You immediately switch from short nine- or twelve-week classes, broken up by midterms and finals, to a forty- or fifty-hour work week spent on one never-ending task, and no summer vacation. Gary will never forget his first year of work. When summer-time came, he was ready to blow out of the office at 11:00 a.m. and head for the mountains. No such luck. The only mountains he got were mountains of work waiting for him at his desk. That first year takes some getting used to.

The above certainly don't represent the only differences between work and college, but they do provide some idea of what you can expect and what will be required of you. While your work life changes substantially, the bigger changes are the changes you have to make in your personal life.

CASE IN POINT
The ultimate adjustment—adjusting to work outside the U.S., by Madeline Kiser

"In May 1984 I was a senior at the University of Michigan. It was a good life. I lived in a sorority with women who liked me even though I wasn't the sorority type (I was an armband wearer, a taker-to-the-streets). I joined out of a mixture of loneliness and curiosity, but despite our differences, my sisters meant something to me.

"I wanted to go out in the world and be a diplomat, someone who sat at a big table translating for people who wouldn't talk; someone who was vital and alive and needed. At twenty-one, I thought these were good things to be. I also wanted, in alphabetical order, to litigate, to philosophize, to travel, especially to Europe and Africa because they were far away. Mostly I wanted to write —every day of my whole life—but I wasn't ready to face this yet; the uncertainty of it terrified me.

"As graduation rushed nearer, I became desperate. I sat in cafés; I pestered parents, professors, and roommates. Late at night, my fellow students and I lay side by side in that cold mixture of fear and fantasy that seizes seniors. What should I do?

" 'Be a professor—you like ideas.'

" '. . . a social worker—you like people.' They were forthright. I wasn't sure. I needed time. On a whim I applied for a scholarship in England and, to my surprise and tremendous relief—relief because this was the closest I had come to finding a job and because these people seemed to want me—won second place. 'Call back in a week,' the recruiter said. 'The winner may change his mind.'

"The winner didn't. Now what? Carol Carter, the author of this book and my best friend in high school, was also searching. Except, unlike me, she had a clear idea what we should do. That's right; what we should do.

" 'We should join the Peace Corps,' she said. 'We'll give two years, come back, then get on with our lives.'

"How I remember these words! I was wearing shorts and sandals and sitting at the counter in my grandmother's kitchen when she said them into her end of the phone. I still think of them! I still think of them because for two whole years in Costa Rica I thought of them as, stooped under a blazing sun, I picked pineapples (they cut); as I struggled through six-hour classes in Costa Rican entomology; as I fell in love with the man I married, a Costa Rican. The long and short of it is that I joined the Peace Corps, while Carol—Carol—went to work in Arizona and later in beautiful, glamorous, dangerous New York.

"Not that I hold anything against her; I don't. The years in Costa Rica were wonderful. Crazy. I got in trouble (traveled to Nicaragua with two men who, as it turns out, were gun runners). The town I worked in—my husband's town—built a 27-kilometer, $300,000 water project in two years.

"I had never met people like the Costa Ricans. To this day, I marvel at their humor and generosity. It is amazing that they allowed a twenty-one-year-old city-slicker foreigner to pretend to teach them anything at all. My official assignment was 'nutrition and gardening.' 'Nutrition?' my mom crackled into the phone. 'What are you going to teach—1,001 recipes for Diet Coke?' I never did teach, though—I just . . . lived there. And they let me. And at the end of two years I came out stronger, happier, and more certain that people are good and life worth living than when I went in.

"It's hard to say how, Stateside, all this translates into jobs. It translates into life. To be sure, the Spanish has come in handy: I am currently associate editor of a small news agency, Pacific News Service, here in San Francisco, not the easiest town in the world in which to launch one's journalistic career; and I got the job in no small part because of my knowledge of the language and of Latin America. I am also a doctoral candidate in the Department of Spanish literature at Stanford—again, the Spanish.

"But the Spanish, and Stanford, and even the reporting, which is the love of my life, pale in comparison to something I now have, wondrously, thankfully: a strength that comes from waiting for Costa Rican buses and waiting for Costa Rican people, who show up, who do not show up, who someday may show up."

The details in your new life

Whether you are in Costa Rica, Pasadena, or Texarkana, adjusting to work is only one part of getting used to post-college life. There are a lot of other things to confront that can provide stress and uncertainty. These things can be stressful because you feel you should have control over them—your money, your friends, where you live. If you already have things in control, you can skip this next section. If not, take some time to read it. This section may save you some major headaches later.

TIPS FOR HANDLING YOUR MONEY

It's easy to get into financial trouble. Some of us are already in financial trouble when we graduate. We've read estimates of as many as one in ten students declaring early bankruptcies because they let their finances go. Gary ought to know; he was almost one of them. In college, credit cards were easy to get, and since expenses are for the most part self-contained—i.e., you know what they are and you usually pay them in lump sums—it was easy to know where you stood. After you graduate, your expenses become much more regular and there are a lot of unanticipated surprises like medical bills and taxes. It's easy to forget a few bills for a few months and find yourself in the credit black hole. However, it's also easy, with regular money coming in, to plan ahead and be responsible.

1. *Budget.* Whether you end up following it or not, the first thing you should do when you get your first job is draw up a budget. It doesn't have to be fancy, just accurate. Try to follow it for the first couple of months and see how it goes. If it is too easy, save more, or pay more of your bills.

A BUDGET WORKSHEET

EXPENSES:

Rent/Renter's insurance

Electric/Water/Heat

Phone

Food

Entertainment

Car payment

Car insurance

Travel costs (to and from work)

Student loans

Clothing
(Starting out, you're likely to need more)

Medical
(Be sure to check your company plan)

Health club fees
(Does your company have a corporate membership?)

Savings

Insurance

Miscellaneous

DIFFERENCE:

INCOME:

Paycheck

Other:

2. *Save money regularly.* You need to have a cushion. If your company has a savings plan, take advantage of it. If it doesn't, plan to set some money aside every pay period, regardless of how much or how little. You probably won't have enough money for any real investing during the first couple of years. That's okay. There are a lot of expenses when you start out: furniture, clothing, visiting your family, etc. You may also want to take a vacation or save for a house. You may need to get your wisdom teeth pulled. In any case, salt something away. There will be times when you wish your cushion was a trampoline.

3. *Pay cash.* Don't borrow a lot, either from banks or on your credit cards, during the first years out of school. A good rule of thumb is that your payments on loans should never exceed twenty percent of your income. Also, by paying cash, you save more; a lot of businesses give bigger discounts for cash payments.

4. *Plan for your taxes.* For the first time, you are probably going to give some cold hard cash to the government. Make sure that you plan ahead: it can be worse than you think. Check with your human resources department and make sure they are taking enough out of your paycheck. It's probably a good idea, unless you are a very disciplined budgeter, to claim none or only one exemption on your W-4 form. This way, come April 15, you'll stand a reasonable chance of getting some money back.

5. *Be a smart consumer.* We aren't suggesting you should spend your weekends clipping coupons, but it is amazing how much money you can save by being sensible. Some examples:

- Shop sales, especially for bigger-ticket items. A good rule is: Don't buy anything you can't eat, unless it is on sale. All department stores, for example, drastically reduce seasonal clothing as the new season nears. Take advantage of their mistakes.
- Eat at home. Eating at restaurants can kill your budget. It's easy to get in the habit of eating out. After a long day's work, the last thing you may want to do is go through the hassle of making dinner.
- Take your lunch to work. We know, it's not the cool thing to do, but it does save a lot of money. Maybe you'll make friends with other lunch-baggers. Or start a new trend.

- Do your own laundry. This can save $10–$20 a week.
- Get a roommate—the easiest and best way to save money.
- Wash your own car.
- Go to the library instead of buying books.
- Rent movies instead of going to the movies.

You get the picture. A lot of this stuff is common sense; it just helps to be reminded of it once in a while. We aren't advocating a hermit-like existence of hunting for bottles you can return or for change in phone booths; we are just urging a little practicality.

Finding a place to live

Your first big change will be in your living situation. If you are already used to living alone or in the company of strangers, this won't be a big deal. But for many of you, moving to a new city, finding your own apartment, house, or roommates will seem a huge task. At the same time, it can be exciting. There is something liberating about getting your own place.

1. *Find it yourself.* You can save a lot of money by avoiding a broker or rental-agency fee. They also tend to try to sell you the largest and most expensive space available. Ask around, or look through the local newspaper. If there is a college in town, check with their posting board.

2. *Money aside, location is the most important consideration.* We have rented some great apartments in bad locations and paid the price. Ask people at your new job about good areas to live in—they are the best source of information. Some things to keep in mind:

Is the area safe? Ask people who live there, and make sure to visit the area in the evening to see if you will feel comfortable and safe coming home late. Is it conveniently located to shopping, recreation, work? Is it quiet?

3. *You can negotiate the lease.* Most people don't realize that renting is a big business. Think about it. A landlord stands to earn $6,000 on a one-year lease of $500 a month. You can usually save yourself $50 to $150 a month, or lower your deposit, just by asking for it. Also keep in mind that the length of your lease is negotiable, and you can often take a longer lease in exchange for less rent.

4. *Take your neighbors and the building into consideration.* The location of your residence is important, but so is the location of your unit within your building. Are you below a party apartment? Near a loud elevator? It's usually a good idea to inspect your prospective home twice, during different times of the day, so you can see what it will be like to live there.

5. *Get the freebies.* A lot of apartment complexes are aiming for a community approach, complete with health clubs, pools, running tracks, and recreation rooms. If these are things you are going to pay for anyway, include them in your rent. It'll make your budget easier.

6. *The roommate question.* People differ on this issue. Having a roommate can save you money and give you someone to hang out with. On the down side, you live with this person all the time, not just nine months out of the year. We would probably caution against a roommate that you didn't already know. There is enough going on in your life without having to try to deal with someone else's problems on a daily basis.

Friends—just do it

Perhaps the most difficult change from college to the working world is the loss of your peer group. Everyone goes a different way after graduation, and for a lot of people it is time to move on and find new friends. It can take some effort to meet people, but you have to do it. If you don't, you'll lose your sanity and sense of self.

We aren't about to tell you where you should find your friends, but there are a lot of not-so-obvious places you may not have thought of:

1. *Sports.* All major cities have formal sporting leagues—softball, soccer, volleyball, etc. A great way to meet new people and stay in shape is to sign on with a league. The city recreation office is a good place to start.

2. *Volunteer.* A lot of people spend time each week doing volunteer work for charitable causes. Larger cities usually have a central agency that lets you sign up for a wide variety of activities, from tutoring to carpentry.

3. *Go back to school.* We've met a lot of people by going back to class. Now that you are through with school, go back and study something you're interested in.

4. *Get a hobby.* You'll laugh, but one of Gary's hobbies is playing competitive bridge (the card game). After he got out of school, he joined the local bridge club. This led to part-time volunteer work helping some of the elderly members in the club. It even turned out that several of the members were actually his clients. Try investigating something you have always wanted to do. It can lead to other opportunities.

5. *The usual suspects.* Of course, there are always the people at work, your friends from college, the people in your building, and religious organizations. Now is the time to stop taking these relationships for granted and see how far you can develop them. You need some solid friends, because you'll have less time to spend with them and your environment is much more stressful.

Making the switch

In a lot of ways, the change from college to work is too quick and too subtle to notice. During the first couple of years, it's easy to get wrapped up in the excitement of your job or a new city and suddenly realize you've been running on empty. Take care of yourself and make sure you have a good comfortable place to live and relax, a good group of friends, and money in the bank. Your personal well-being is harder to tune up if it's been ignored for a while.

1. *Keep your mind active.* Even though you're about to graduate or have graduated, don't let your education stop. This doesn't mean you should take night classes every evening of the week. Just make a point of keeping your mind in shape. It will help you on the job, but, most important, it will make you a more interested and interesting person.

2. *Stay informed.* We both live in New York City, so we rely on *The New York Times* for information. Wherever you live, there's bound to be several newspapers available. And don't just read the sports section. If you prefer watching TV to keep up-to-date, there are a number of good news programs at almost any time of the day or night. You can see live coverage of the news as it happens, from Moscow to Rio to Tokyo. Keep up on what's happening in the world—economically, politically, socially.

3. *Read.* One of our favorite journalists, Pultizer Prize winner Anna Quindlen, describes reading, for her, as "life unwrapped, a way of understanding the world and understanding myself through both the unknown and the everyday." Whether you read *Forbes* or *Fortune* or *A Farewell to Arms*, reading expands your mind and causes you to think in new and different ways. You'll probably feel that you've done all the reading you want in the last four years, but now you can read something you choose!

One of the most enjoyable ways to make sure you read at least one book a month is to form or join a reading club. Carol has been in a reading club for the past three years. Each person gets to choose a book, which everyone reads. The group has dinner and discusses what they've read. Each member of the group interprets the book differently, which makes for some very impassioned debates! We've read books as diverse as Joseph Conrad's *Heart of Darkness* and Barbara Kingsolver's *Animal Dreams*.

Keep the balance right

An important principle to remember in your first year out is to keep your balance. At the difficult points, it's very easy to forget what made you the person you are. You can become obsessed with work and suddenly find yourself spending sixty hours a week at the office. It's natural to want to do well, but if your life is out of balance, it will eventually catch up with you. As John Leche, an actor we interviewed, said, "It's easy to lose perspective in your first year. I felt as if I had lost mine. I'm reminded of what Woody Allen said to Diane Keaton in *Annie Hall*: 'Here, let me take off my shirt, so you can feel my heart with your foot.' "

Keep your shirt on and your senses about you.

The Self-Portrait:

Understanding Yourself

Why not spend some time in determining what is worthwhile for us, and then go after that?
—William Ross

You are asked not to exert extraordinary skill, but to place extraordinary trust in the skill you already possess.
—Harvey Oxenhorn

Management 101

Uncertainty. That's the most accurate word Jean Godfrey could use to describe the months up to her graduation and starting out on her first job. In college she had four roommates and classes she had come to understand. She knew where she fit in and where her limits were.

Now she was newly married (to Gary) and moving to Cincinnati, Ohio, a city she'd never even visited, into an apartment she'd never seen. She had no job, only a vague idea that her American Studies degree from the University of Colorado might be a good background for advertising. She had no money, no occupation, and no friends in the new town. Really, she had no identity. She had to define one for herself.

So, when after a month of job hunting, she found a job as the only copywriter for a small family-owned advertising agency, that cloud of uncertainty temporarily disappeared. But another one, perhaps more ominous, moved right in to take its place.

Her new job brought a whole new series of challenges. Since she was the only copywriter, she had to produce a wide variety of pieces, from radio and TV commercials to newsletters to print ads. She had to answer to three or four account executives (some related to the owner).

She had to meet and make deadlines or face a loss of business. Most of these things she had never done before.

On top of this, there were the adjustments to living with someone, the infamous first year of marriage. Finances, cars, insurance needed to be coped with: household chores outlined and schedules coordinated. Friends needed to be made and the social circle rounded out for both people. It seemed at times that Jean was the cruise director, ship's captain, and engineer all rolled into one.

Your first year after college may not be as topsy-turvy as Jean's, but you will be making adjustments. You'll have to manage your activities, your friends and family, your health, your hobbies, your expenses, your time, and all the key people in your life. Suddenly, everything you used to take for granted—your meals, your laundry, your money—is up for grabs and not automatically taken care of.

At work, the picture will be the same. Companies have embarked on a downsizing movement, and unlike other adjustments to the economy, this one has been particularly hard on middle management because so many layers of management have been trimmed away. At first glance, you might think that downsizing has little effect on a new employee such as yourself. In fact, beginning workers are expected to be more and more self-sufficient. There simply aren't as many managers to go around. You'll have to rely more on yourself and your immediate colleagues for the support and guidance that used to come from above.

The trick to keeping your sanity in the face of all this sudden responsibility—before work, at work, and after work—is consciously and consistently to manage yourself. Know what you're good at and bad at, what you like and dislike, and what you can realistically expect to accomplish. Try to mold this self-awareness into a plan, a set of assumptions you can work by. Jean and Gary used to spend hours on the porch talking about situations at work and how best to handle them in light of their strengths and weaknesses.

In Carol's first year on the job, she had to learn to take work in stride. She cared very much about doing a great job, but sometimes she put too much of herself into it. At times, this kept her from gaining the perspective she needed to deal effectively with a situation. Learning not to take everything personally was an important part of developing business maturity.

CASE IN POINT
A cartoon character takes the long road

Ed Koren, the artist who did the cover for this book, knew since he was very young that he wanted to be an illustrator. The following is an excerpt from an interview with Koren in *Columbia College Today*:

Q: *What advice would you give a young cartoonist?*

A: I think this has to be the hardest area to break into. I know personally maybe six or seven people trying—mature artists who keep making the rounds of syndicates and find that there are closed doors and somewhat opaque welcomes to their efforts. What advice? I wouldn't give any, except if you want to draw, if it's really your passion, do it. But don't expect a whole lot to happen. If you are funny and satirical, and if you are good at expressing that graphically, then do it, see what happens in your life. It's like writing poetry; you can't base your decision on the marketplace.

Q: *How did you get started?*

A: Well, I was pretty reticent about it, because then, as now, there wasn't a whole lot of opportunity. For me, *The New Yorker* was it: I was always attracted to that kind of openness to expressing things. What happened was that when I was in college I kept sending stuff to *The New Yorker* and I got veiled, discreet encouragement. They'd say, "Well, we think it holds promise for us maybe someday." It was just enough—I was quite elated even by that crumb being dropped on my rather empty plate. Meanwhile, I did other things—I became a printmaker, which I studied and ended up teaching; I worked at Columbia University Press for a year, doing advertising—while all the time submitting things to *The New Yorker*. At a certain point, four or five years after I graduated, I started working more consistently on cartoons and illustrations. Bit by bit by bit, a couple of drawings were submitted to magazines and then one was published. Little breaks like that were crumbs—delicious, but not a meal.

Understanding yourself

Koren understood some very important things about himself: he is passionate about drawing cartoons, he was committed enough to stick it out until he began to get the breaks, and he was realistic about his lack of experience initially. He built steadily on the talent he had.

"Knowing my downfalls was the main reason for my success," says Julie Doig, who was promoted three times, to unit manager at Procter & Gamble. She's right! Every single person has his or her share of strengths and weaknesses. The first step you should take is to spend some quality time analyzing yourself and your situation. Upper management values people who have a realistic understanding of who they are, what they can do, and where they want to go. Why? Because this is exactly the attitude someone in upper management has to take when making strategic decisions for the organization.

It may take a while to understand yourself. Entire lifetimes don't necessarily yield lucidity. There are some tests that might help indicate broader patterns in your personality. One such test, the Myers-Briggs Inventory, asks you to answer a series of questions and then rates you according to a scale and a set of criteria:

Extraversion
Sensing
Thinking
Judging
Introversion
Intuition
Feeling
Perception

The survey asks you to quickly answer questions like:

When you go somewhere for the day, would you rather
———Plan what you will do and when or
———Just go

Do you more often let
———Your heart rule your head? or
———Your head rule your heart?

For a more detailed description of this test, write to Consulting Psychologists Press, Inc., 577 College Avenue, Palo Alto, California 94306.

Personal qualities and job performance

Your innate talents or qualities are those things that come naturally. You do them without thinking. Other qualities can be learned—determine their importance, and make a conscious effort to cultivate them.

For example, one of Carol's innate abilities is interacting with people. She has always been intrigued by people and befriends everyone wherever she goes. By recognizing this talent early on, Carol was able to apply it to her work in sales and marketing. People love to talk to Carol, and they like to work with people they like.

But there was a flip side to her talent. Because she's such a people person, Carol tends to give everyone the benefit of the doubt—she sees the good and can ignore the bad. This optimism was fine when Carol was in school or even in her first year on the job, but when it came time to manage people and get involved in more complicated negotiations, she had to learn to be more realistic. Being too Pollyannaish hurts you. Learning to be critical in her appraisal of people was an important step for Carol.

▶ *Test yourself*

What are your natural strengths?

What are your natural weaknesses?

How do you think your strengths will help you on the job?

How can you prevent your weaknesses from being a problem on the job?

Personal characteristics on the job

How are your strengths and weaknesses likely to fit into your first job? Following are a few characteristics mentioned as important by the people we've interviewed. Most likely, you'll share a number of them or, as you read, come to learn a little more about yourself. These characteristics are intended as a frame of reference, not a be-all, end-all. They will exist in varying degrees in any given job, so look at them and figure out how they apply to you.

Intensity

How driven are you? Do you believe in doing whatever it takes, as fast as you can, to get something done? Do you work in starts and fits of intensity, or do you operate at a consistent level? If you are a low-intensity person or used to short periods of intensity, work will be a major adjustment. Jobs involve varying levels of intensity, but in general they call for more prolonged periods of intensity than does school. For the most part, there are no final exams you can cram for, no make-up tests, and no incompletes offered.

The stress monster

If you are accustomed to a high level of intensity, you will have to work hard to temper your natural tendency to overachieve with an occasional need to step back and regroup. In a job, there is less time to rest and recharge. The four months of vacation suddenly become two weeks, and very few people can go full-speed fifty weeks a year. Learn to manage your intensity level so you can apply it hard in the crunch times. If you expect too much too soon, you may find yourself blowing up over minor incidents. Being intense—caring about your work and the quality of it—is an important attribute, but being too wound up too much of the time can be harmful to your health and, over time, will reduce productivity.

Advice for the stress monster

So, what should you do if you're prone to high stress? Learn to cut yourself some slack. Don't expect too much from yourself too fast. Learn to pace yourself, and learn to unwind. Remember, too, that, except in extreme cases, stress is a state of mind. Some people thrive on the same stress that drives you crazy. Sometimes people who are too results-oriented have to make a goal of relaxing. It may sound silly, but learning to unwind can be as difficult for active people as learning to take on new challenges can be for less driven people.

Laid-back, too laid-back

If you are the kind of person who can always think of a million reasons not to do something, or if you prefer to take things slow and steady, you will have to learn to gear up. All jobs require some level of intensity. Companies do not expect every employee to be an overachiever, but they do expect employees to achieve. And with more people chasing fewer jobs, companies are willing to cut non-performers sooner.

▶ *Test yourself*

Think back to the last time you were under a lot of stress. For most people, the month or two before graduation is a particularly harried time. You are juggling finals with job interviews, thinking about moving, and making plans for graduation. How did you handle this time? Was it a big deal? Did you let some things drop? Were you particularly edgy? If you came out of it with flying colors, then you probably thrive on stress. You'll need to control yourself at work, making sure you don't burn out. On the other hand, if you had a great deal of trouble, you should anticipate more of the same and try to develop some coping strategies.

Problem-solving and critical-thinking skills

If nothing else, college was supposed to teach you to think. Unfortunately, some people get out of a spoon-fed memorization-driven environment and don't know how to think through major issues in their life or even small aspects of a job assignment. There are many different styles of thinking. Some people start with the big picture and then fit the little pieces into place, while others put together little pieces before they begin to see the big picture. It doesn't necessarily matter whether you are better at deductive or at inductive reasoning, but it is important to remember how you look at things.

The nineties will reward people who can develop solid critical thinking skills to help them wade through the vast amount of information available. For example, three years ago, the average textbook sales representative at Prentice Hall needed only two basic sales tools—a car and a catalogue. Now, the entire ordering system has been computerized and a sales rep is expected to keep detailed ordering histories on all his or her customers, instead of relying on memory. Sales reps have voice-mail and electronic mail. The number of books they sell has increased by over two thousand titles and expanded into a number of new and unfamiliar markets. Top that off with a restructuring that eliminated a level of management, and you have a very different picture. And college publishing is a very slow industry. In other industries, such as communications and computer software and hardware, change is the only constant.

▶ Test yourself

It's your third week in a new job selling commercial fabrics to offices in New Hampshire, Maine, and Vermont. You've just finished sales training, and it is time for you to hit the road and try to get some business. In training, they told you your first step should be to make an itinerary: what accounts and what cities you should visit and when. Unfortunately, the previous representative left poor records and now works for a competitor. Fortunately, your boss used to work in this territory a few years ago.

Your ask your boss for help, and she shrugs and says, "I have a meeting in an hour. I'll give you until then."

What are some of the questions you should ask her?

Write them down:

This exercise is tough but typical. By using a little logic, you were probably able to come up with questions like: What area or cities are experiencing the biggest commercial real estate growth right now? Who is my largest current customer? Who is my competitor's largest customer? When you had the territory, how did you work it?

There are a number of other questions you could ask on topics ranging from travel recommendations to the personalities of the buyers at your accounts. It would be nice to know all the answers, but obviously you can't expect to walk in and ace your first assignment. No one you work for should expect that, either. What they can expect is for you to think.

Learn to ask questions and listen to the answers. Try to think conceptually about how problems can be solved. Learn how to organize information in a way that helps you make decisions.

Most important, remember that the key is categorizing the information, assimilating it, and analyzing it. Of course, you need to have some basic facts and figures about your job in your head, but don't try to memorize everything.

Decision-making and independent judgment

Solving problems is one thing; deciding what to do with your solution is another. If you are a careful decision-maker—that is, if you tend to weigh all the evidence and analyze the pros and cons before acting, your decisions are likely to be sound. If you are impulsive and decide too quickly, the result may not always be reliable.

One of Gary's natural tendencies is to make decisions quickly, sometimes with little consultation. For the most part, this works out fine. But once in a while, in haste, he'll overlook an important component. For example, he recently decided to buy new computers for his department. He purchased two top-of-the-line computers and a printer, perfect for the job, at a good price, and managed to get the order through in record time. Unfortunately, he failed to note that they weren't compatible with his current machines. He had to hold the order at the last minute, to change it. If he had asked around, his co-workers would have warned him, and no time would have been lost.

The nineties will place greater decision-making demands on individuals. There will be more decisions for the average person to make, and the sheer volume of information available will complicate the process. It will be difficult to make decisions by yourself, but involving others could bog you down. How the decisions are made is what will matter, so focus on understanding and improving your own decision-making skills.

Leigh Talmage, an international bond and debt trader, argues that the hardest thing in one's first job is to walk that fine line between independent decision-making and being a team player. "In your first job, you don't have the freedom to make decisions and use independent judgment. You have to learn how to present your views and gut feelings on what should and should not be done without offending your colleagues or boss. You must be a team player."

TIPS FOR MANAGING THE DECISION-MAKING PROCESS

1. *Involve others in your important decisions.* Be careful not to let too many cooks spoil the broth and lead you to second-guess your instinct.

2. *Develop a formal decision-making process.* What do you do when you buy a car? Do you shop around, compute the various loan payments on paper, etc.? Or do you just decide you want a particular type of car and go buy it?

3. *Decide on a time frame for your decision.* Oftentimes, when you need to make a decision, just deciding is more important than thinking it to death.

Taking and giving directions

In your first job, you will probably be taking more orders than you give. That's the definition of entry-level. Jacqueline Adams, an administrative aide at the International Bank, seconds that. "In reality, your first job will be one of taking direction. For the most part, you must learn to take orders without taking the process personally. Try to leave 'personally' out of the office. As you progress in your career, you will learn to give orders and delegate responsibility with sensitivity if you are able to leave your ego out of it."

Whether or not you are in a position where you formally give orders, you will give more directions than you are used to, officially or unofficially influencing the lives of your customers or co-workers. And unlike in a part-time or summer job, you need to develop long-term working relationships, both upward—to your boss—and horizontally

—to your co-workers. This is a difficult change for people used to running their own show, so take a moment to consider how you work with people.

The good soldier

If you are good at following directions and if you do everything you are told, you will be a delight to manage. What you will need to push yourself to do, however, is to learn to take risks with your ideas and initiatives. Since your tendency may be to wait until someone says that it is okay to do something, you may miss the moment of opportunity, because you fail to act quickly enough. You'll also have to learn to assert yourself more, since, for your long-term career, you'll have to come up with good ideas and persuade others to your way of thinking.

The maverick

The opposite of the good soldier is the maverick—the irreverent, idea-generating employee who almost always has a better plan. If you are a maverick, then you probably dislike getting too many directions and don't want any eyes peering over your shoulder to make sure you're getting things done. You need a long leash. Since most companies and managers have a hard time managing mavericks, you'll have to work hard to rein yourself in a bit. Don't stifle your creativity; just learn to play by the rules. You don't have to be a total conformist, but you do have to play within the broader guidelines of the company.

CASE IN POINT
An environmental planner who manages
her environment

Enid Lotstein, an environmental planner, tries to balance her soldier and maverick tendencies: "When I am given an assignment at work, I develop an opinion about what our decision should be, a strategy or a conclusion based on the data or evidence I have. I present my conclusion along with the supporting evidence to my supervisor or project manager. Sometimes he agrees with me and sometimes he does not. If at that point he disagrees with me, in most cases it is out of my hands and it's time to let go of the issue.

I believe that I am taking risks and initiatives with my ideas by developing an independent opinion and stating it even if I may meet with disagreement.

"I want to contrast this with the approach of some of my co-workers. One of my colleagues has an opinion about everything. The problem is that Ed sees details without seeing the bigger issues, and he doesn't recognize when to set aside his opinions, defer to other team partners in order to finish an assignment in a timely manner. He seems to disagree over any point just for the sake of argument. For example, he may be told by one of the project managers that the client doesn't agree with him, to which he'll retort, 'Tell the client he is wrong!' Recently he stated that a particular project was disorganized and that everyone involved should sit down and have a meeting to discuss it. Well, there just wasn't time for ten people to sit down. He fought the tide so much that when a choice was made about whom to involve marginally or fully in the responsibilities for the project, he was left on the fringe. That's why I think it is good to have an opinion and to be a good soldier. Timing is everything."

▶ *Test yourself*

As an assistant loan officer you have responsibility for screening small business loans and making recommendations on whether or not they should be approved. You also have the power to approve loans without supervisory input up to $10,000. However, since you are just starting out, you have been showing every loan to your boss, just to make sure you are doing the right thing.

Recently, you received an application for a promising restaurant business in a good location. You interviewed the applicant and checked his references and everything came up clean, except that the applicant had no previous credit experience. After some thought, you decided to approve the loan, knowing beforehand that it was the type of loan your boss wouldn't approve. Would you approve the loan and skip your boss (is it in your power)? Would you show your boss the loan application and argue for approval, or would you reject the loan outright and save yourself the trouble?

We suggest discussing the matter with your boss. If you feel strongly that, based on your impressions of the applicant, you could make an exception to the rule, then it is important to make a case. If your manager does not agree, you have to trust his or her seniority and judgment. It is generally a bad idea to make a decision that you know your boss would not approve.

Initiative and results

Once you're out working, people will expect you to be self-propelled and get results. If you are lucky, you'll have a boss or co-worker with the time to answer your questions, but at some point you must or will assume responsibility and make your own decisions.

Charles Heines, an attorney, says: "If you want to be the best, you have to push your self-made boundaries and go for the higher level. Staying in a safe and comfortable job is not bad, but it will prevent you from achieving what you can and desire to do. What occurs in most instances is that it is not competition or the marketplace that hinders our progress. Usually, we ourselves set the limits of what we can and cannot do."

The longer you are out of school, the more your confidence will grow. Remember what you were like as a freshman? Don't talk yourself into being insecure. You got the job. Now what kind of initiative do you have?

▸ Test yourself

Do you take action on your own without being told what to do? Do you wait for people to tell you what to do?

Are you results-oriented? Do you focus on outcomes?

Do you concentrate on a goal and then commit yourself to it?

Do you believe you can always find a solution to a problem, no matter how complex or challenging?

Perfectionism

Every job requires accuracy. You should never spell a client's name incorrectly in a letter or forget to verify the information in an estimate of future sales. However, accuracy and perfection are not interchangeable concepts. Perfection can be sacrificed in the cause of speed; accuracy cannot. It's important to know how driven you are by perfectionism. In your first job you may have even more of a tendency to want to get things perfect. This can bog you down.

An anecdote about the famous post-Impressionist artist Paul Cézanne illustrates the silliness of striving for perfection. Cézanne was commissioned to do a portrait by his good friend the art dealer Ambroise Vollard. The meticulous Cézanne made his friend sit for drawings, sketches, and painting 115 different times before he was finished. After he was done, a critic asked Cézanne what he thought of the painting. All Cézanne could say was: "I am not entirely displeased with the shirt front." A great artist has time for this level of detail. On your first job there are many more practical considerations.

"Perfection is normally self-imposed and adds additional stress to your job," says Brian Sahd, who works for the Urban Assembly, a non-profit agency. "You should try to eliminate the perception of perfection from your workplace, it does not exist. You should strive for high quality and accuracy in your work, not perfection."

Excellence will always stand out on the job, and it's important to want to do things thoroughly. But you also need to get things done on time.

▶ *Test yourself*

Do you cross all your *t*'s and dot all your *i*'s?

Do you get upset when something is not done perfectly, or according to your system?

Do you give yourself credit for doing the best job you could under the time constraints?

Curiosity

Curiosity is one of the primary characteristics for long-term success on the job. Why? Because people who are hungry to learn typically know more over a period of time than those who are uninterested. If you want to learn all about your job, your industry, and how other industries relate to your own, you'll be a more valuable player.

People with an appetite to learn are forever expanding their knowledge base and their options. Ross Martin, a professional model, says: "I think a person develops curiosity and inquisitiveness throughout his or her career. Too often, people forget about being challenged and stretched at work. It is one of the most important aspects of a job, since you spend more time in your life working than you do anything else besides sleep. Whether you are a truck driver, a surgeon, or a financial expert, you always want to increase your knowledge. Ask questions and show your curiosity."

Humor

A Presidential press conference is the epitome of stress. Hordes of eager reporters are alert for a slip-up or the one right answer. Jimmy Carter is known as one of our more soft-spoken Presidents, so few people realize how funny he can be. Since he is a Southern Baptist, Carter was constantly asked about moral issues. "How would you feel if you were told that your daughter was having an affair?" a reporter asked. "Shocked and overwhelmed," answered Carter, adding, "But then, she's only seven years old."

Humor is one of the greatest trump cards in business. It allows people to make light of otherwise grave situations and helps people to laugh at themselves as well as at a tough problem. You don't have to be humorous to have a sense of humor. Most people would starve as stand-up comedians and yet they can help people to see things more clearly by breaking the seriousness of work with appropriate asides, analogies, or witticisms.

If you take yourself too seriously, people will find it tedious to be around you. On the other hand, don't become a jokester; people won't take you seriously. Learn how to step back from people and situations. If you can get the best out of yourself and out of others, you'll end up solving more problems, you'll be more productive, and people will enjoy working with you.

Peter Jude, a controller for a mid-sized bank and an avid Star Trek fan, once found himself in a situation that allowed him to combine his work and pleasure. "I was preparing for a particularly excruciating bank board meeting in which I knew our very solemn and distinguished president would expect me to discuss detailed figures on the subject of twenty-four-hour ATM machines. Toward the end of the meeting, the president asked me about the revenue possibilities for ATM machines. He expected me to have little information, but this was a way to get me going on the project. I rose swiftly to the challenge, put on my best Spock imitation, and replied: 'I cannot be precisely accurate, sir, but according to my calculations, I believe the bank could expect a first-year intake of one hundred Quatludes.' The room broke up, relieved after the long meeting. A little humor can go a long way. But remember to earn the right to be funny, by knowing what you are talking about."

Personality

We all have our own style, our own strengths and weaknesses. These personality traits and ways of thinking are important to keep in mind in the world of work. While an employer will have many qualified people who are capable of completing any one assignment, each person will have a different personality which will make him or her more or less effective at a particular task. Knowing your strengths and weaknesses will enable you to position yourself to take on those responsibilities at which you are best. It is also the first step to strengthening the weak areas, which you must do in order to succeed.

Most important, you should never second-guess yourself. "Don't hide your natural abilities," says James Conover, an administrative assistant in Washington, D.C. "Don't try to be someone you're not. If you're true to yourself, your career will advance naturally."

David Slocum, a screenwriter in New York City, agrees: "You have to be honest with yourself." He likes to recall the words of the humorist Dorothy Parker: "Hollywood is the only place where you could die from encouragement." For David, this means separating the wheat from the chaff and having a realistic picture of yourself. "Screenwriting is like anything else, you have to commit yourself a hundred percent, but first, know what you are really capable of doing."

The Achilles heel

Another word of caution: Keep in mind that your greatest strengths can also be your greatest weaknesses.

Napoleon Bonaparte is a great example. Barely over five feet tall and born to a large, poor family of less than royal origin (actually, they were dirt farmers from Corsica), he used his tremendous physical and mental drive to build the largest empire in Europe. His charisma and ambition fueled over ten straight years of victory and conquest. But in the end it was his greatest strengths, his drive and ambition, that proved his downfall. They led him to overextend himself, to fool himself into thinking he could conquer not just Europe but all of Russia. His army was decimated by the Russian winter. They surrendered and Napoleon was sent into exile. If only he had owned a copy of *Graduating into the Nineties!*

As you think about yourself and the new experiences in your life, pause once in a while to ask yourself some questions: What is difficult? What do you enjoy? What gives you a sense of satisfaction? What worries you? How many of these things are within your control? How can you better accept the things that are not within your control?

Go easy on yourself. You are making many adjustments at once. If there are aspects of your life, your job, or yourself that you don't understand, give yourself time. What you are experiencing is completely normal. Remind yourself of that when the going gets tough. And remember that self-understanding is a process that happens over time. You have to experience situations before you can interpret what they mean. A few years from now, what we've discussed in this chapter may make a lot more sense. Until then, it will be an advantage to have been introduced to these concepts.

The Telephoto Lens:

Managing Yourself and

Setting Priorities

Being good in business is the most fascinating type of art.   *—Andy Warhol*

Where is the knowledge we have lost in information.   *—T. S. Eliot*

If you don't know where you're going, you'll probably wind up somewhere else.
      —Lawrence Peters

"Wine, wine, wine." That's the inside joke that Kathy Ransom would throw at her friend Leslie Lauren every time Leslie complained about not knowing what to do next. Kathy and Leslie graduated together from the University of California, Davis, and both worked at a major California winery. Kathy was a chemist and Leslie was a systems analyst.

For Kathy, figuring out what to do each day was easy. All her wines were checked chemically on a chronological basis, so when she came to work in the morning, she knew exactly what to do. There were six or seven chemists with similar jobs, and accuracy was the major criterion by which she was judged, so she always knew where she stood. If she did well, she could hope someday to manage the group, but beyond that, her opportunities were limited, unless she changed industries.

For Leslie, it was entirely different. When she took the job, the term "systems analyst" sounded dignified, but after two or three months of helping people set up their computers, she had quite a different opinion. Each day she had to meet with her manager and co-workers and struggle to split up her time appropriately. There were many urgent pleas for help, from all parts of the company, all seemingly equally important.

On the upside, Leslie's group was rapidly growing to match the pace of the technological growth of the company. In the few months that she had been there, she had seen her group grow from six analysts to eight, and her boss had been promoted to director of information systems. There was talk of computerizing the entire company, and she was at the heart of the action. If things didn't work out for her, she could easily move to another industry.

What do Leslie and Kathy have in common, aside from having gone to the same school and working at the same company? Certainly, they could commiserate about the dead-end nature of Kathy's job and the lack of control in Leslie's. Wine, wine, wine. We all need to do a little of that from time to time. But what they really shared is a difficulty in getting their priorities straight. For Leslie, it was day-to-day. For Kathy, it was the long-term outlook, two or three years down the road.

Getting organized

Whether short-term or long-term, setting priorities is central to everything you do. If you don't know what you want to get done and when, you won't get it done. Marinella Moscheni, an administrator for the Economic Research Bureau, thinks that budgeting your time is the most important thing a recent graduate can learn. "Smart time management and goal setting are the keys to productive performance—and sanity on the job."

In your first year, you'll be trying to strike a delicate balance. At times you may feel completely out of control despite your best efforts to organize, prioritize, and keep yourself composed. It's perfectly normal. It's okay to ask yourself, "Am I spending my time on the right things?" In fact, it is the most important question you can ask.

Before you dare to be better, before you set priorities, you need to be organized. We've all been exposed to disorganized people. The worst case we ever saw was a man who never really understood his job in the first place. He could not focus, he could not make order out of the chaos, and he could not properly follow up on anything he had to do. Working with him was like entering a great abyss—you felt you were being sucked in, but you felt helpless about getting out.

Admittedly, there are disorganized geniuses. One of them is the head of our market research department. Although his office is an unbelievable mix of papers and stacks of computer printouts, he always knows where everything is. He keeps it all in his head. But don't be fooled, he is an exception.

For the more common folks like us, it's necessary to keep track of things. If organization is not your strong suit, it's time to form new habits. One of the best places to start is with a senior colleague who has the same job as you. He or she's been around long enough to handle the flow of work and information and can tell you what is and isn't important. You don't have to become a neatnik, you just have to learn to keep track of things. It will make life easier in the long run.

1. Write things down.
2. Start a filing system.
3. Handle pieces of paper only once.
4. Learn to throw things away.
5. Keep a date and address book.

These things need no commentary. They are straightforward, but it is amazing how many people skip the basics. "If employees just behave normally," says Connie McGuire, "they'll do fine on the job." Connie, who is personnel manager for a large insurance company, comments on what amazing excuses people have for not doing their work properly or on time. Or for not coming to work on time, or not coming to work at all. "Think about the messages you send to others in the small things that you do," advises Connie. "Have some common sense, and be courteous."

Connie makes an important point. If you are sloppy or lazy in your approach to a job, it will affect your work. You may not even realize it. So, think about your habits and behavior. Err on the side of being overly concerned, and you'll keep yourself in check.

Setting priorities

Learning to set priorities—and learning to think through what is important for you to do each day and each week—is the main thing you need to master early in your career. (Some of the other things you'll learn about in this book are icing on the cake, but this is not one of them.)

Evelyn Morenzi, who works for a non-profit planning corporation, offers sage advice: "Don't think about things too much, just do them.

Each job situation will be different, but one thing will always be the same: your boss will want you to get the job done as quickly and accurately as possible. The first thing you must do is prioritize your tasks. Then write them down in order of priority. You should expect that there will be times when everything will be important and you should count on burning the midnight oil to get those important things done.''

What are priorities? They are your running list—in your head or on paper—of what you need to do, in order of importance. Oftentimes, it is difficult to tell just what is the most important thing you can be doing. That's why the best-organized people review their priorities on a daily and weekly basis. They add to their list, they cross things off as they go, and they set new priorities as necessary.

Below is a sample list. There is also a blank for you to fill in your priorities for tomorrow and this week.

MONDAY

1. Write weekly summary
2. Meet with purchaser
3. Confirm sales goals
4. Have lunch with applicant
5. Meet with boss to discuss project
6. Follow up with JPMyers

Phone calls:

1. ANL
2. John Nash
3. Videodisc company

Check off things as you finish them. (Very few actions provide greater satisfaction than crossing off items on a "To Do" list!) At the end of the day, take fifteen minutes to make up your list for the next day while work is still fresh on your mind. That way, you don't have to think about the following day's chores all night. At the end of each week, think through the next week and month. Having a system of priorities will give you great comfort.

CASE IN POINT
When the job gets to be too much

Sometimes, no matter how much planning you do, you can be overtaken by stress. Raj Sammanin's first job out of college was as a paralegal for a large corporate law firm in San Francisco. The first few weeks went okay. Raj was given several research assignments and completed each within the designated time frame.

"After a while I was given increasingly complex projects which I needed to complete in very short periods of time. At one time I was working directly with two partners and four associates. They all wanted my time, and they all wanted their requests yesterday."

As time went on, Raj felt more and more swamped. Admittedly, he wasn't good at breaking down his tasks—and fears—in his mind. After six months on the job, he felt completely overwhelmed. His stress level was at an all-time high.

"Finally, I went to our firm's personnel department to get advice," says Raj. "I honestly didn't know if I should stay in the job or quit. I've always been a stick-with-it kind of person, but for the first time I had real doubts about myself."

At the suggestion of a personnel counselor, Raj sought professional help. Fortunately, his law firm's health policy covered seventy-five percent of his expenses. Within a month, Raj's head was much more clear, and he was back to working at full speed. With the help of a therapist, he learned to break down his tasks, analyze his relationships, and manage his fears. He learned how to communicate—with himself and with others—which in itself was a tremendous release of stress.

Raj's is an extreme case, but at times just about everyone feels as he did. These are the times when you feel like quitting or walking straight out of your office and onto the beach. Sometimes, taking a breather is a good idea, but for the most part you can minimize overload by planning ahead.

However, there are also some jobs that may not be the right fit. That happens. It's okay. Gary wouldn't be a good airline pilot. Carol would not be a good marine biologist. If you get into a job that is not right for you, seek objective help before getting out of the situation completely. Explain your predicament to a friend, sibling, parent, former teacher, or anyone else whose judgment you trust.

Short-term goals

Prioritizing is one way to control stress. Another way to stay focused is to set goals for yourself. We like to think of short-term goals as covering anywhere from a six- to a twelve-month period. Setting short-term goals will help you break down what you have to do, so that you have a mental game plan.

After you have been on the job for a few weeks and begin to have a better sense of the work environment—the structure of your job and the opportunities and challenges—you can begin to set some short-term goals for yourself. You're probably familiar with the goal-setting process. Everyone has goals, but we don't always arrive at them through a formal process. You had or have a goal to get a job, to finish school, to get good grades, but you probably didn't tack your goals on your wall.

TIPS FOR SETTING GOOD GOALS

1. *Make them reasonable goals at the top end of what you think you can do.* They should stretch you without breaking you.

If you are in sales, it is probably not reasonable to suggest you'll double the sales in your territory in one year. It doesn't happen very often. At the same time, don't set goals that are part of your everyday routine. Holding sales at the same level as last year wouldn't be a sufficient goal in most cases—it's your job!

2. *Make them measurable goals.* Otherwise, you won't be able to tell how well you've done. Being a better person, for example, is not a measurable goal.

3. *Make them multi-faceted goals.* Have goals for all the various functions in your job as well as in your personal life. This way, you'll develop a broader vision in your job and you can maintain a balance between your job and your personal life.

4. *Write your goals down and don't be afraid to revise them.* Goals can change. One of Gary's personal goals last year was to run a marathon. He did that in November and found himself needing another goal, so he added the goal of keeping in shape for the rest of the year. (He didn't make that one!)

5. *Evaluate yourself periodically.* Be your own judge. Keep track of how you think you're doing, and take action to improve your performance where necessary. You should do your own self-appraisal before you and your manager sit down to discuss his or her point of view.

Setting formal performance objectives

We've talked generally about your goals, but we haven't made a distinction between your personal goals and those your organization has in mind. Most likely, your organization has some specific things they would like you to accomplish.

Whether your company has a formal goal/performance objective process or not, it's a good idea for you to write down your professional goals for the year, review them with your manager, and refer to them each month. Goals help you maintain a focus and serve as concrete measures of success throughout the year. If you accomplish all your goals and a couple more to boot, then you will have extended the requirements of your job. If you manage really to re-create your job, to make it better in a number of visible ways, then you may be given an outstanding evaluation and a good raise. But this rarely happens in the first few years. Be patient with yourself. Aim high, do your best, but don't be disappointed. Things take time.

On the following page, list your performance objectives—your work goals—for this year. We've listed a sample for you to follow:

Performance objectives—first year

Job: Assistant Manager, Department Store X
Goals:

1. Increase sales by 15 percent on last year's base.
2. Hold turnover to 25 percent.
3. Remake the image of the junior-teenage line of clothing. Develop a strategy with local advertisers to increase market share with this audience.

4. Streamline/reorganize restaurant menu to include more healthy foods. Advertise food specials each Wednesday along with merchandise items in paper.

Now it's your turn.

Performance objectives

The five most important things I must accomplish this year are:

1.
2.
3.
4.
5.

Skills I need to develop:

_____   _____
Employee signature   Manager's signature

Common goals allow you and your manager to agree on what's expected of you. If you don't have a clear idea of what you're supposed to accomplish, it's hard to know if you're doing the right thing throughout the year.

If you don't have a formal goal-setting process, write down what you think your goals are and show them to your manager. Does he or she agree? Disagree? What would your manager add or delete?

Hang on to your goals and look at them periodically. Are you where you want to be? Ahead? Behind? If you are behind, what can you do to catch up? How can you get additional help?

One year later, you'll be able to look at your goals before you and your manager have your performance review. Most managers are interested in your honest appraisal of your own work before they let you know what they think.

The broad view: long-term goals

In addition to priorities, short-term goals, and performance objectives, it's a good idea to have a long-term plan for your life—say, three to five years down the road. "Nothing stops the thief of time," they say. Before you know it, you'll be wondering why you didn't accomplish all that you wanted.

Whether you've just completed your senior year or you've been out of school and on the job for a few years, the best way to set goals is by looking back at the last year, at where you came from. As Santayana said, "Those who cannot remember the past are condemned to repeat it."

Carol's older brother, David, is a good example. He changed his life's priorities after getting his Master's degree in England. A journalist by trade, David turned down job offers in San Diego, New York, and Washington to return to his hometown of Tucson. He worked at the paper there a few years as business editor and, as a hobby, he committed himself to a long-time interest—restoring the downtown "barrios" of Tucson.

After a few years, David left his job at the paper to begin his own building and restoration business in the barrio. "My own business gives me the lifestyle and flexibility I need with my family. Plus, I'm helping to build and shape an area in the community which I really believe in," says David.

Ken Elgarten's first job out of school was as a financial analyst for First Boston. "I didn't have many options when I started college and I wanted to make sure that when I graduated I could make the most out of each opportunity. I wanted the past to be a help, not a hindrance."

Take a moment to see how your past can help. Give a written response to the following questions. Be honest.

The two most important things I accomplished last year were:

1.

2.

Two things I wanted to accomplish but didn't:

1.

2.

The two most enjoyable experiences I had were:

1.

2.

The two most difficult, character-building experiences were:

1.

2.

On the whole, I rate the year as:

1. One of the best I've had
2. Very good
3. Good
4. A learning experience
5. A waste—looking forward to next year

What I would have done differently:

What I learned:

It may feel odd the first time you do this exercise. We hope that thinking through these questions will help you to understand yourself and make improvements on the job where necessary as you go.

Are there any patterns in what you've written? Which of the things you wrote down were within your control? Reviewing what has happened is the first step to effective goal-setting. Once you have a clear idea of where you've been, you'll best be able to determine where you're going. Where do you want to be in five years? We've heard this question so much that we forget how important it really is. Your first job should help you reach your long-term goals.

"To get the most out of your first job, you should think about how it can help you build a long-term vision of your life," says Ellwood Hopkins about his job as an assistant director for the Megacities Project, an organization that focuses on the exchange of technology among the megacities of the world: New York, Mexico City, Tokyo, São Paulo, London, and New Delhi. "Your first job should have meaning in terms of your past investments and your future dreams."

CASE IN POINT
Values clarification, by Cynthia Nordberg

"**I** wanted a college education so that I could get a well-paying job. Initially, I believed in that fallacy of the American Dream that prosperity cures all ills.

"However, during my years at college, my values began to change. Religion began to play a larger role in my immediate life. I began to ask: What does God want from my life? I switched my major from business to rehabilitation and decided to work for an urban ministry when I graduated.

"After two years, I was made director of promotions. Fund raising became a separate department, with its own director. At first, I loved my job. Gradually, however, I began to long for more hands-on work with people. Sitting behind a computer and giving presentations to businesses and churches wasn't my original goal for a lifelong career. But the skills I acquired served me well in my next job with a non-profit organization specializing in youth ministries.

"With a non-profit organization, you need business savvy and public-relations abilities just as in other professions. It also helps to enjoy working with a broad variety of people. You'll talk with the president of a large corporation as well as the local junk collector. Both deserve the same respect. The key to helping people is through building relationships, with one person at a time.

"Most of the kids in our program are from single-parent homes with a substance abuser in the family. Because of the myriad of problems, the children lack parenting and they crave individual attention. We believe in quality, not quantity, although quality goes hand in hand with doing the best job you can. We started with eight children and now have twenty-five. Our goals are twofold: discipleship and development.

"Ours is a very grass-roots approach because we believe in indigenous leadership. A single mom in our neighborhood coordinates the tutoring program, and most of our volunteers are from the community. If you are going to work within a culture different from your own, you must understand their perspective and their needs. One of the biggest mistakes I've seen social workers make is to ignore cultural dynamics and arrogantly assert that they know what their clients need, without asking their opinions. Remember, people don't care how much you know until they know how much you care.

"Whenever I talk with a young person about careers, I challenge him or her to ask what it is they really value. Asking this question will help you determine what you should be doing with your life.

"Downtown, we have the Chicago Board of Trade, where futures are invested. I also believe in investing in futures: the futures of people. Sure, I sometimes wish I lived in a suburban home with a backyard and much less people interaction. My life would probably be more comfortable, but I doubt it would be half as meaningful or as real."

It took Cynthia several years to realize her goals, but her short-term goal of changing her major from business to social work had serious long-term effects. Likewise, her first job switch from a larger, more corporate non-profit agency to a smaller agency gave her the foundation she needed to reach her long-term goal of starting a new agency.

You have several years to think about and change the priorities of your life. For many of us, they change every few years, based on the circumstances and on our values. The important thing now is not to know exactly what you want to do, but to be thinking ahead, keeping your eyes and ears open, learning what you can from your current situation.

▸ *Test yourself*

Make a list of your professional and personal goals for the next two years.

Look these over. Are any professional goals in conflict with your personal goals? Are these ambitious but realistic goals? Don't set yourself up for failure by setting goals that are too far from your reach. On the other hand, don't sell yourself short by setting goals which are too easy.

Think about why you set these goals. What kinds of things are important to you? Why will you feel good about yourself after accomplishing these goals?

Use these goals as a benchmark over the next couple of years. Looking at your goals a few years later is a way of keeping score.

Life goals: the long, long term

When Carol was interviewing for jobs during her senior year of college, one recruiter asked her what she would like to be doing in five years and in ten years. The five-year question was fair enough, but the ten-year question was absurd. Sure, she could say, "I'd like to be with the same company, be promoted several times, and be a regional manager." The truth is she, like most people, had absolutely no idea.

In fact, if you had told Carol that very day that ten years later she would be living in New York, working in publishing, and managing a marketing department, she would have thought you were crazy.

In Carol's early twenties, she didn't think much about the long, long term because everything seemed quite immediate. The first time she thought about the long term was at her tenth-year high school reunion, when she was suddenly struck by how long it had been since she graduated. She felt sort of old, for the first time. Her friends at the reunion all looked different. They had lost the youthful innocence that they had in the reunion slide show, which featured photographs from their high school days.

Now that Carol is approaching thirty, she thinks of things differently. Ten years ago, she was willing to go any length for her career. She also jumped at the opportunity to travel, to explore and do somewhat risky things. While she will always be an adventurer at heart, now she is weighing different things. Where she lives is more important to her than it was earlier. Quality of life—liking her job and having enough time to pursue other interests—has risen on her priority list.

For Gary, things were different. He got married right after college and had to think of many things Carol didn't. He and his wife both had to compromise, too. At times, she moved because of his work. Other times, he moved because of her work. Their long-term thinking is now affected by the prospect of starting a family. Your decisions depend on economic considerations as well as on what you'd like personally.

In the first few years out of school, most people aren't preoccupied with the long term. That's okay. Unless you get married, start a family, and buy a house right after college, your twenties can and should be more carefree. You may want to take it easy on the job so that you can spend more time with friends. Or you may want to work hard, get on the promotion track, and then go to graduate school. Some people who work very diligently in their twenties can spend more time in their thirties reaping the benefits of their hard work. Don't forget to save some money while you're at it.

CASE IN POINT
Gigi Veguilla and the non-traditional path

Not being the conventional type, Gigi chose—by default, really—to get her education, not at a state university, but at the school of hard knocks. "It will all pan out, it always has," thought Gigi.

By the age of twenty-six, Gigi had three children, half a year of college, a bad marriage, and no money. She was the typical single mother, working, going full-time to a community college, teaching her children, taking care of the home, and working out (racketball and weights). Let your mind wander as you imagine a young woman with a baby hanging on her side, teaching two other children to read, while taking care of all household duties. To top things off, she was raised in a chaotic, eccentric home. Anyone in his right mind would have recommended that she give up—she had too many strikes against her.

Fortunately, when she found herself floundering in the dire straits of life, she decided to fight the current and swim upstream. The cruel realization hit her: this was her life and no one was going to rescue her. She had to make some choices. Did she want the best she could provide for her children? Did she have to juggle a career to support the family? Did she still have to keep up with all her commitments and responsibilities? The answer to all these questions was yes. And unbelievably, during this time she learned to play the piano, kept up her guitar playing, and wrote a full-scale musical as well as other incidental music.

She is doing it but, as she says, "It takes military genius, mercy from God and man, and a lot of push." And no, she's not yet close to being where she wants to be. But she has learned to understand the process of change, and she is learning to be patient with herself and with her circumstances.

Gigi has been through a lot for someone so young. But her understanding of herself and her situation has enabled her to deal successfully with adversity. She has a lot to be proud of.

"Moderation in all things," said Terence. Like Gigi, you have to learn to be patient in understanding yourself and in setting goals to become better. Start with one or two realistic goals and build from there. To keep your motivation high, remind yourself of what's gone well in your recent past. The change you want to effect will happen in due time, as long as you are committed to it.

To manage yourself well, you have to continually reevaluate what is important. The ability to prioritize—to know what things are essential, what things are marginally important, and what things are icing on the cake—is critical. Decide which things matter the most and focus on those. This is a good rule of thumb in both your personal life and your business life. Second, be flexible enough to recognize when you have to change your course of action for a better plan. Life is in a continual state of flux—we can't be static in our thoughts or actions.

For the long term, it's important to focus and invest time and energy into those things which really matter. You can only do that by keeping your goals in sight and by measuring your current progress against them. You also have to ask yourself continually why you have the goals you do and if they should change based on other things you'd like to accomplish. You have to manage your life.

The Group Shot:

Managing Relationships in

Your Company

When one is wrapped up in oneself, he or she makes a pretty small package.
—John Ruskin

Give all the credit away.   *—John Wooden*

When you get right down to the root of the meaning of the word "succeed," you will
find it simply means to follow through.   *—F. W. Nichol*

Jack Leavenworth's nickname around the office was "Lava" Jack. He
was always fiery hot, and if you got in his way, he ran right over you.
He never bothered to seek anyone's opinion, and if you tried to offer
one, he ignored you and restated his own. In meetings, he grew dis-
tracted and bored when the topic wasn't centered on him. If you had
a problem, it was your own, but if he had one, the world needed to
know. Jack really didn't fit in and didn't care if he did.

How can someone like that survive in the business world? Well, Jack
was one of the most successful real estate sales people in the city. He
was driven, aggressive, and when it came to his customers, he was
everyone's best friend. There wasn't anything he wouldn't do to make
them happy. It was strange to watch him talk on the phone, it seemed
like another personality was at work: caring, happy, interested.

He leased so much commercial real estate that the partners were
willing to overlook his inability to work with others in the office. At
the same time, they realized that Jack would never move up and that
at any moment he could get too out of control and have a negative
effect on the performance of others. He was a very profitable time
bomb.

Jack's type is a dying breed in the organizations of the nineties. In today's smaller, flatter organizations, successful relationships at work will be critical. Mutual respect based on mutual gain will be the watchword as organizations expect more and more from fewer people. Teamwork will be critical, since it will be less clear who is in charge. If you can't learn to manage the small group relationship, you will have a hard time being successful.

Build a big picture first

The first step to working successfully within an organization is to know its general structure—where you and your peers, manager, department fit in the overall scheme of things. Marge Bellock, former vice president of product management at Discover Card, agrees. "Be a generalist, so people can envision you in different areas. Specialists become obsolete." Alisha Whitacre, director of management and organizational development at Colgate-Palmolive, seconds that. "In our organization, a strategic business sense is replacing narrow specialization as the key way of thinking. A broader approach to business is an unusual quality and those who have it really stand out."

▶ *Test yourself*

Draw an organizational chart. If you don't know who fits in where, ask your co-workers. Start with whatever is easiest, probably your unit or department. If you work for a gigantic company, do only your division. Your chart could look something like the one on the facing page.

Why is this information important? For one thing, it helps you to understand the chain of command so you can follow up on your work flow easier. It also lets you know exactly who has power. Offices are political battlegrounds, and titles don't always mean what they seem. One of the most powerful people at Prentice Hall is the assistant to the president. Although she doesn't manage a huge number of people, her opinions and advice are heard by the president directly. She is the gatekeeper who decides who does and doesn't see him.

William Childs, a computer consultant in Chicago, defines gatekeepers as those key assistants or aides who get things done behind the scenes. "Behind every source of power there is too often a neglected

RANNER PAPER COMPANY

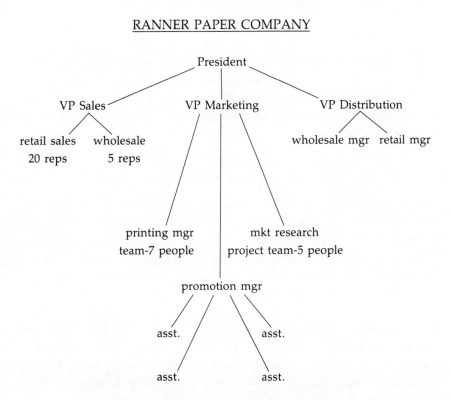

President

VP Sales   VP Marketing   VP Distribution

retail sales   wholesale   wholesale mgr   retail mgr
20 reps   5 reps

printing mgr   mkt research
team-7 people   project team-5 people

promotion mgr

asst.   asst.

asst.   asst.

*My job—specializing in new product development
total employees = 86

gatekeeper seeking attention. It pays to know who and where these people are." We think it pays to know who everyone is.

Learn the process

After you feel comfortable with the "who," turn your attention to the "what." Develop a thorough knowledge of exactly what your organization does to make money: how they create their product, how they sell it, and how they pay their bills, and who does all those things. Knowing this process inside and out takes some people the better part of a career. Starting out, we're only suggesting you have a general idea. A broad understanding of the flow of your company puts your job in perspective and will help you follow up on your work. It also provides clues as to who your important contacts will be.

▶ *Test yourself*

Pick one of your organizaton's major products or services and trace it from start to finish. Be as detailed as possible and ask as many people as you can to verify your information. This way, you'll build new relationships as well as gain knowledge. For the most part, people love to tell you what they do. No one ever asks!

Get to know the organization through its people

The single most important resource your organization offers you here is people, their experience and skill. Make the rounds and start learning from your co-workers. Start by simply getting to know people. Nancy Cetorito, manager of compensation and benefits at Homedeco, an in-home nursing and therapy service, attributes a lot of her success simply to "making a point of getting involved with other people in the organization and their work and walking around and saying hello." Anita Brick, a partner in Decision Dynamics, agrees. "Invisible people get cut. It is critical to talk to everyone, if only to say hello. People who make it to the top get enough people on their side to get things done."

Saying Hi as a way to do well on the job? Sound crazy? It's not. Devoting time to your co-workers is incredibly important, and it is something most people don't do. Upper management places high value on broad-based interpersonal and communication skills, because in most organizations, unless there is a crisis, there isn't time for management to concern itself with operational issues such as the way the mail is delivered or the phone answered. By stepping in to fill a void, you can learn to get things done and at the same time give yourself a link to the top.

Ask everyone questions. Remember how you were when you were a kid, always asking questions, like why is the sky blue, or why does the doorbell ring? It's time to get in a similar frame of mind. Steve Branson, regional sales coordinator at Carnation Company, did. "Absorb as much information as possible from all people." Collar everyone, from the mailroom personnel to the receptionist in other departments. You will be astonished by the fact that knowing their name, what job they do, and the issues surrounding their job makes you important.

"Be respectful of other people's jobs. Business is a two-way street," says Stacy Niesen, director of special projects for BMT Publications, an organization which specializes in trade magazines. "If you can offer

Agrilot Agriculture
Primary business: food processing, stringbeans

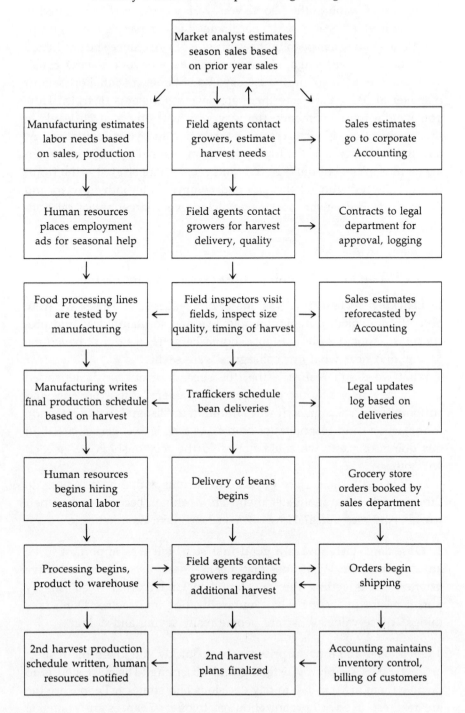

Market analyst estimates season sales based on prior year sales

Manufacturing estimates labor needs based on sales, production

Field agents contact growers, estimate harvest needs

Sales estimates go to corporate Accounting

Human resources places employment ads for seasonal help

Field agents contact growers for harvest delivery, quality

Contracts to legal department for approval, logging

Food processing lines are tested by manufacturing

Field inspectors visit fields, inspect size quality, timing of harvest

Sales estimates reforecasted by Accounting

Manufacturing writes final production schedule based on harvest

Traffickers schedule bean deliveries

Legal updates log based on deliveries

Human resources begins hiring seasonal labor

Delivery of beans begins

Grocery store orders booked by sales department

Processing begins, product to warehouse

Field agents contact growers regarding additional harvest

Orders begin shipping

2nd harvest production schedule written, human resources notified

2nd harvest plans finalized

Accounting maintains inventory control, billing of customers something of value to the people you work with, they'll be inspired to work with you." Stacy, who coordinates the company's focus groups and trade shows, has been in the same line of work since she graduated from college six years ago. Her motto is: Treat everyone as your equal.

"I hate the word subordinate," says Ron Stamer, regional operations manager at 3M. "Each day there are several moments of truth. How you handle these moments, the way you treat others at all levels in the organization, is what creates your honor and your reputation. At 3M, the customer is at the top of the organizational pyramid and management is at the bottom." At 3M (and everywhere else), it is the frontline employees who fill the gap and communicate both upward and downward. The newer workers actually have a larger set of relationships to manage!

The keys: listening, observing, and involving

1. Listening. At first, this was one of our biggest challenges: we were both strong-willed, outgoing people. We had so many ideas and preconceived notions of how things should be done, we didn't have time to stop and hear what our colleagues were saying.

What we didn't realize is that the success of our work depended heavily on how we fit into our work environment—the experience and support of our colleagues. It was important to "listen," to pay attention to the actions and responses of others. As long as we were focused on our points of view, we could not build the relationships we needed with others.

Look beneath the surface in your interactions with others. Whom do they respect? What motivates them? How can you become part of their world? And vice versa? How can you help them do a better job?

2. Observing. Listening is a good first step, but it is important to be an active listener. What does that mean? These days, the term "active listener" starts getting thrown around in kindergarten. Well, simply put, it means analyzing what you are hearing and seeing. Don't take things at face value. What are people really saying and doing?

3. Involving. You'll be surprised at how quickly you'll win the respect of your peers simply by listening and observing. The next step is to involve them in your day-to-day decisions and strategy. People are the greatest resource your organization has to offer. Chances are, someone at your organization has done your job and done it well. (You better hope so, or you may need a new job soon!) Use them. Ask them for advice and help as often as is convenient. Don't waste their time, have a clear set of questions, but ask often. You'll do your job better.

CASE IN POINT
Todd O'Connor and the tough road of the teacher

"**M**ost people don't realize that teaching is one of the most relationship-intensive jobs that exists," says Todd O'Connor, a substitute teacher in Salem, Oregon. "Not only do I have to manage a hundred kids a day, but I have to be prepared to handle their relationships with their parents, their relationships with each other, and their relationships with other teachers and coaches. I also have to manage my own relationships with other colleagues, the principal, and counselors.

"It gets really complex when a student isn't doing well. When I see a student isn't performing well, I have to decide how to talk to him or her. What could be the reasons for his or her poor grades or behavior? It could be something at home, drugs, a girlfriend or boyfriend. It's easy to assume you have the right answer, so I have to do a lot of listening and observing before I say anything. Then I need to be very careful about what I say and when I say it.

"If my discussion with the student doesn't work, I usually call the parents. Often, the parents will be divorced or separated, so I have to be careful about whom I call first. I also can't put the blame strictly on the student, myself, or the parents. I have to be constructive and cooperative, if I am going to have any chance at success.

"If the parents can't help, I then decide on what type of disciplinary action, if any, would be appropriate. At most schools, references—i.e., giving one of your students to a different authority—reflect poorly on the referring teacher. I have to have good documentation that I have tried everything, talked to everyone, tried to work it out. At any point in the whole process, one slip of the tongue or one missed clue can lead to failure."

Office politics: where are your key relationships?

In Todd's case, there are many key players and a lot of personal politics to wade through. He needs to keep his eyes and ears open at all times and focus on the relationships that are important to him. Most situations will be like that; there will be some people who play a more critical role in your work life than others.

Getting to know everyone you can is a good start, but as time goes on, it will become apparent that you need to have a separate strategy for managing a few key people. Start by remembering the framework and boundaries. Refer back to your organizational and flow charts. Who are the main people you'll interact with every day? Which of those people have the greatest effect on your job?

"Understand your office environment," says Jerry Johnson, who is a zoning examiner for the Bureau of Standards and Appeals. "Most people new on the job don't realize it, but the office is a very political place. This is vastly different from college. How one deals with politics and other people is just as important as how well one does the job. It can greatly influence whether you succeed or fail."

"Getting to know the people on your job is just as important as the subject matter," says Richard Stevens, a bond trader in New York. "It is whom you know, not just what you know. I'm not saying be ruthless—for lack of a better word—but your relationship with those in power should develop as systematically as your mastery of the subject you are dealing with."

But don't let politics get in the way of getting your job done. For most of you, becoming overly involved in the affairs of your co-workers can be a distraction and a detraction. Jane Dobson, an environmental lawyer, suggests focusing primarily on the task at hand. "If you spend too much time getting involved in what other people are doing, you will not be able to focus on your job and do good work. My advice is to focus on your work and establish a reputation for developing a good product. Of course, you need to know where you fit in the organization, but if you aren't doing your job, it won't matter whom you know."

Jane brings up a good point: relationships take time. How many key relationships are you managing? If you are managing a lot, learn to share your time equally. We all have a tendency to pay the most attention to those relationships which are easiest, even though they may not be the most important. If you are managing a smaller number of relationships, learn to maximize them without burning out or getting too personal. Think of your relationships as a bank account. You can withdraw only after you have put money in. Sometimes you'll need to take out and give loans, but strive to maintain a decent balance.

Working in small groups or teams

Managing relationships with your peers and key contacts has always been important, but the late eighties and nineties have seen a tremendous change in the way organizations tackle their problems. The team approach is growing and this structure requires a different set of skills. In the past, organizations were primarily hierarchical, military in nature. Everyone had his or her job, orders came from the top, orders were executed. Now a shift is on to an opposite approach: people are organized into small teams and are given problems for the team to figure out. Responsibilities are not as clearly divided, and people are being forced to work more closely with each other.

Working with people to get things done can be one of the most enjoyable aspects of the job, if you like people. But not everyone is "people prone." Some feel more comfortable working with facts and figures; some feel more comfortable analyzing, researching, or processing information.

Do all people-prone men and women make good team players? Not necessarily. In the example that opened this chapter, "Lava" Jack may have worked well with his customers, but he was trouble for his co-workers. To be a good team player, you have to adjust your focus from yourself to the group. You have to learn to swallow your pride, sharpen your listening skills, and open your mind to others' thoughts. In our formula of listening, observing, and involving, observing is the most important ingredient.

TIPS FOR BECOMING A TEAM PLAYER

1. *Develop a "team" mentality.* Before you can be a good team player, you need to develop a team attitude. Learn to think about others, their motivations and their potential, as a group. Think of yourself as both a leader and a participant and know the difference between the two. Also learn when it's appropriate to shift from following to leading. Watch how people in the group interact and be careful in taking sides.

2. *Participate in team activities.* Some of the best team players in business develop their skills outside the office—on the volleyball courts, in the driving range, or in the bowling alley. Others build team skills through volunteer leagues, clubs, or activities like sailing which involve their hobbies. There are usually group activities sponsored at work. If you need to learn to cooperate, it's better to start by joining a preexisting group. This way, you'll be forced to fit in.

3. *Take pride in the team.* As corny as it sounds, "team spirit" goes a long way to success. You need to jump right in and support your co-workers individually as well as a whole.

Contributing to team success

How do you think you—the individual contributor—can foster team success? Think about those things which others do to motivate you. What makes you interested in a project? What maintains your interest? How is your behavior affected by how others relate to you? If you played on a sports team when you were younger, or sang in a choir, or participated in a theater group, you'll understand the impact individuals can have on the overall, successful outcome for a group. Teamwork on the job is very similar.

CASE IN POINT
From assistant to hygienist
in less than a year

John Langeless's first job after college was as a dental receptionist. He wanted ultimately to become a dental hygienist, but getting his foot in the door was an important step while he took evening classes to get certified.

"I worked in a large office of eight dentists. Each had at least one assistant. Since I was used to the structure of college, especially the organizations I was in, I wanted to put people together and set some goals. I found out what I could do to help each of the other assistants. Since I was the most recent employee, I volunteered to take all the off-times for lunch. Since I was new, I needed to gain their respect. Doing things to help them out would help to build a relationship."

Eventually, John established a rapport with almost every assistant. He became the self-appointed coordinator among them. He organized the lunch and vacation schedules. Most of all, he helped the assistants to take pride in themselves—to go beyond the ordinary confines of the designated job. After a while, a few of the dentists noticed that John was making a difference among the employees and the patients.

After a few months, while John was still in school, three of the dentists asked him if he would work for them once he was certified. They could tell he had potential to do the job well and that he could build and develop relationships. Because John was an effective team player, chances are that he would build loyalty among the patients.

Traps to avoid

John did things right, but it wasn't easy. It is easy to make mistakes in dealing with people. People can be emotional, fragile, and irrational. Haven't we all been? Oftentimes, you need to put on the kid gloves and take care to say the right thing at the right time. The following are common traps that you should try to avoid.

1. *Forming cliques.* There are a number of reasons to avoid factions within your department or company. First, it sends a strong statement to everyone outside your group—namely, that at some level they don't belong. It also makes you extremely vulnerable to downswings in opinion. If one member of your clique fails, it will reflect on the group as a whole. Finally, things change! The group that looks good today can end up losing out tomorrow.

2. *Sex and race are off-limits.* Under no circumstances do discussions or comments about race or sex belong in the office. For many of us, the question is not an easy one. What constitutes sexual or racial discrimination? It isn't always a clear-cut case of physical harassment or use of bigoted terms. It can simply be an offhand comment, an attitude, or a casual glance the wrong way. Such behavior is never appropriate, even behind closed doors, even at a company function.

► *Test yourself: what is sexual discrimination?*

You are a new employee and the only woman in your group of five staff accountants. The men have been pretty decent to you for the first six months. Sure, there were the usual comments about whether or not you were going out with anyone, and shop talk centered on male topics, but nothing came up that you couldn't handle.

Recently, however, you have sensed a growing rift between you and one of your colleagues who disagrees on the proper categorization for a key client's liabilities. To make matters worse, the client prefers you over your colleague, though the client doesn't necessarily agree that your categorization is correct. There have been several controversial meetings on the subject.

In the last meeting, your colleague began framing his argument entirely in sports analogies, something he knew you wouldn't understand. You asked him to explain and he looked to the others (all men) and rolled his eyes and picked up right where he left off. Is this discrimination? How would you handle it? Go learn the sport? Confront him in front of your colleagues?

We suggest setting up a separate meeting alone with the person whose behavior was insulting. In an unemotional, straightforward way, explain your position. If the person is unreasonable or if he continues the annoying behavior, you can file an official complaint with your human resources department. Sexual discrimination or harassment is grounds for dismissal in most major companies.

If you work for a small company, tell your manager. If senior management does not take action to reprimand the person and stop the behavior, you may want to look for another job.

3. *Passing judgment.* Try to avoid being your brother's keeper. You aren't your peers' manager, so don't act as if you were. Avoid judging them to yourself and others. One of the worst mistakes Gary ever made was making some bad comments about the effectiveness of one of his co-workers. Imagine Gary's surprise when he found out a month later that the co-worker was his new boss. Not only had Gary been wrong in his initial judgments, but now he ran the risk of having his comments get back to him. Ouch!

4. *Brown-nosing.* Hardly anyone is despised more than the brown-noser. Don't try too hard to make yourself known. You'll end up alienating your co-workers and eventually upper management. It is

okay to let people know how you are doing, but do it when it is appropriate, in your monthly report, your group meeting or presentation.

5. *Gossiping, or breaking a trust.* Be prudent about the grapevine. When people ask you not to say something, don't! You may think it's okay to tell one close friend, but your close friend probably has a close friend, and so on. Winning trust is an honor, but you'll be surprised how little you'll know if you break that trust just once. Guard against personal gossip as well as gossip about co-workers.

CASE IN POINT
Loose lips sink ships, by Greg Ferro

"It's amazing how important the 'little things' that we say really are. My first job out of school was working for a prosperous auto dealership in a large Southwestern city. After several months of duty, I was put in charge of all the bank errands—deposits, withdrawals, contracts, etc. Over time, I came to know the various bank employees quite well. We would joke, laugh, and generally have a good time whenever I came in. Unfortunately, this casual acquaintanceship would cause me considerable grief at one point.

"When I entered the bank on that fateful day, everybody looked tired and cranky. After the usual complaints about the weather, one of the tellers told me her car had been repossessed by the bank because of lack of payment. I sympathized, commenting that the entire economy was doing badly and that even my dealership wasn't selling cars as well as it had in the past. This idle chatter continued for five more minutes, until I left and returned to work. I did not realize that my slightly mendacious remark about the dealership, which I had made more for something to say than for any other reason, would almost get me fired by Friday.

"When I returned from lunch the next day, the dealership was in chaos. Our bank, completely out of the blue, had sent people over to audit our financial records and do a complete inventory check. Similar scenes were taking place at all the owner's dealerships throughout the state. Our owner was infuriated by the bank's behavior and set out to find the reason. I helped out as much as I could, thinking how much I would like to meet the people responsible for all this excess work and give them a piece of my mind.

"On Friday afternoon, right before I was to go home, my boss called me into his office. While walking there, I remember thinking to myself, 'It's about time for me to get a raise.' When I arrived, I was surprised to see not only my boss but the general manager and the owner of the dealership. (The owner, who had given me the job originally, was my godfather and lived about a hundred miles away.) All three were staring at me. I knew I was in some sort of deep trouble, but I didn't have the slightest clue as to why.

"They asked me if I knew why I had been called in. I responded no. Then the owner asked if I had noticed all the extra work that had had to be done in the dealership in the past few days. Of course I responded yes, adding that it was a pain and wondering why the bank had done this. The owner, who had known me all my life, looked me in the eyes and said 'You.'

"Stunned, I remember asking how, weakly, not believing that I could have been the cause of something this major. The owner ignored my question and asked me why I would tell the bank that the dealership was going bankrupt: a complete and utter lie. More confused than ever, I said that I'd never said such a thing, or ever implied it. He then said he had proof that I had said it; the president of the bank, located in a city 150 miles away, had told him this morning that that was the reason for all the audits.

"As they waited, I tried to think of something that I had said recently that could have been interpreted this way.

"It seems that on Wednesday, after I had commiserated on the car-repo story, another teller, who'd only half heard the conversation, thought we weren't selling any cars at all and assumed we were going bankrupt. She told her boss what she thought I had said, not bothering to verify either with me or with any of her co-workers. Her boss told the bank manager, who called his manager, who then called the vice president of the bank long-distance in the capital city, who then notified the president. The president then called his advisors, who ordered a full audit of the assets the bank co-owned/financed with the owner.

"I think it was both my look of total incredulity and the fact that the owner knew me personally which saved my job. When I finally left work, I went to my parents' house to discuss what I had done. After listening to my saga, my mom looked at me for a moment and then said: 'Loose lips sink ships.' Do they ever! My flapping mouth cost the owner over $20,000. Naturally, the auditors found nothing, but the accounting fees and stress alone kept everyone tense for the rest of the month. Amazingly enough for me, after a serious tongue lashing regarding what I say and when, the incident was dropped and never mentioned to the other employees.

"The moral of this story is that in the working world people are always listening. Always assume that if you say something to someone, your boss or your competition is going to know about it. Also, assume that people are going to mishear or misinterpret what you are saying. Think before you speak, and when you do, clarify your words! If I had only been aware of the value of this seemingly common-sense statement, I would have saved myself and others an incredible amount of grief and cash."

---

6. *Personal discussions belong at home.* It is hard to find anyone to blame in Greg's story, but one person you may not have considered culpable was the very first bank teller, the one who told Greg the bank had repossessed her car. It was this comment that led Greg to make his seemingly innocent remark. Somehow, her comment made Greg feel that he had to say something to make her feel better. When personal discussions enter the workplace, you open up a can of worms.

"Keep personal discussions to yourself," says Andy Reiss, an architect in New York City. "Keep everything on a polite business level. It's okay to have friends at work, but holding personal discussions can backfire and lead to suspected favoritism and clique-forming." Or, as in Greg's case, to near-disaster.

7. *Socializing at work.* What about making friends at work? Is that something to avoid? Generally, we think it is good, natural, and unavoidable. Sometimes the best way to get to know someone is away from work, on a social basis. Many important business decisions, and some of the most innovative ideas, have come up over a restaurant table, not in the boardroom.

When people are having fun, they open up, relax, and show more of themselves. Maybe it's a Friday afternoon Happy Hour, maybe you teach a colleague how to play tennis or invite one or two people over to your house for dinner. You chose the company you work for, and part of that decision was probably based on the people. Don't be afraid to get to know your colleagues outside of work.

Of course, there is a fine line between socializing with people at work and forming the cliques we talked about earlier. You have to strike a balance between your circle of friends outside of work and your co-workers. After all, if everyone at work knows everything about you, it can make work and your personal life awkward. Find the balance that's right for you.

CASE IN POINT
Discretion is the better part of valor

LeeAnne began her first full-time job in a credit training program for Mellon Bank in Pittsburgh. One of the people who interviewed her for the position was Marcos. He was the only one who suggested that the company not hire her. Despite his poor initial judgment, however, she got the job.

After several months, Marcos became LeeAnne's manager. The initial lack of chemistry soon abated. The two made a good work team; they respected each other and they accomplished a lot together.

A few months later, their relationship developed beyond the purely professional level. They began dating, which was awkward for both of them because of their professional relationship.

"We decided not to make our relationship public," says Lee-Anne, "even after Marcos was transferred to our office in London. We discussed it and felt that, professionally, it was better for our colleagues not to know about our personal situation. For one, we did not want to be judged unfairly by our managers and colleagues. Two, we clearly didn't want the office to know about our personal lives—it was our business and ours alone. Three, we didn't know if our relationship would last. We didn't want to announce our relationship because we thought it would jeopardize our jobs and possibly our relationship."

In this day and age, with people spending so much time on the job, it is possible that you will meet someone at work whom you will start to date. Keep the above scenario in mind. It's better to be cautious, not cavalier, in matters of the heart.

Working with your manager

Your relationship with your manager is most important and will count the most in your career. Try to get off to a good start and develop the relationship as time goes on.

Your manager won't be your best friend: that's not his role. It is his responsibility to train and develop you so that you grow, contribute, and remain challenged on the job. In the best of circumstances, you will develop mutual respect and admiration for each other, which will in turn further your productivity and motivation.

"There are two types of management style," says Henry deLogier, president of Resort Management of America. "You may have a totally autocratic manager who will produce exceptional short-term results. On the other hand, you may have a laissez-faire manager who is more popular but less productive with a group of people. Whichever type of manager you work for, err on the side of self-discipline. If you try to be your own manager, you'll solve more problems in the most responsible ways."

"Learn to manage up," advises Kent Daniel, who worked for Philip Morris as a strategic market planning associate right after school. "You have to manage your boss and your boss's boss. Much of business is about perception as well as action. If you can do your job well and also help to make your boss's job easier, you'll be an asset."

What is it like to have a great manager? After two or three months at his job, Gary felt his relationship with his manager John had grown to the point where he could approach him for advice on any subject, no matter how compromising, and expect to be given logical, unbiased advice. For example, although Gary was among his most valuable employees, John would not hesitate to give him advice on how to pursue opportunities in other divisions in the company. He also allowed Gary a wide range of control over his work, but still made sure Gary was performing within his strategic plan (which Gary helped draw up). He was an excellent manager, because he realized that management is not a one-way dialogue; you have to manage your relationship with your manager as much as he or she manages you.

Some people never reach this point with their managers. "If you don't have too much supervision, don't be surprised," says Jennifer Adaire, an associate marketing manager for Pepsi in Purchase, New York. "You have to learn to add value on your own." For those with great initiative, this can be a blessing in disguise. You can still figure out the parameters of your relationship—what's expected, what's required—and leave the inspiration and rapport-building to others, mentors or colleagues who are close to you within the company. Over time you may be surprised to find that a meaningful relationship can develop with someone who seemed an unlikely partner at the outset. Be patient.

CASE IN POINT
Mark Joseph, conference coordinator

Mark's first boss was a perfectionist. She had the reputation of being very hard to work for. She was highly organized and intimidating. "My boss was merciless about keeping an organized office. She was also relentless about keeping track of work in progress, even after I was apparently finished with a task. I was totally intimidated at the beginning of my tenure with her."

After working closely with her, Mark learned that he really wasn't focused and was only modestly organized. "During the first year, I came to have ultimate respect and admiration for her. When I examined my strengths and weaknesses and compared them to hers, I was able to see how to develop my job skills. I learned to cope with a demanding person. And although I will never be as neurotically organized as she is, I believe that I am much better at my job because I have worked for her. I am more focused and much more organized than when I started my career. Most important, by learning to manage her, I learned to manage myself."

TIPS FOR WORKING WITH YOUR MANAGER

1. *Be objective.* Understand your manager's position relative to the company and your position relative to others he or she manages.

How many people does your manager manage? The more, the less time you'll have to spend with her.

Does she have additional responsibilities apart from managing?

Are you her most difficult employee, her newest, the employee with the most responsibility? Your manager has to prioritize her time accordingly. Where do you fit?

2. *Communicate.* Don't be afraid to tell your manager of your successes, failures, and goals. He can't help you if he doesn't know what you want.

3. *Liberate.* Find ways to help him do his job better. If he is an autocratic manager, help him build team rapport. If he is laissez-faire, help define some concrete goals your group can achieve. Your goal should be to magnify the team's effort while still getting your job done.

Mentors

During the course of your work, you will probably develop a close affiliation with someone who is one step ahead of you. If it doesn't come naturally, you'll need to force the issue by finding yourself a mentor, someone whose brain you can pick, from whom you can solicit suggestions on how you can do your job better. Perhaps there is a project that you can work on together. Maybe she (or he) can tell you what she did in her previous job which better prepared her for her current position.

CASE IN POINT
A first mentor

When Carol was a sales representative in Phoenix, Arizona, she was fortunate enough to work in the field with a woman, Robin Baliszewski, who later became one of her mentors. Robin gave Carol many helpful tips during their day together and in the evening, when they went out for dinner, they really enjoyed themselves. Carol liked and respected her as a person and as a professional.

Robin became Carol's champion. After a productive day together, Robin went back to the home office and told her boss that he should work with Carol. Two weeks later, Carol got an unexpected call from his secretary saying that he would be changing his schedule to work with her for two days. Carol had three days to prepare for this trip. Since Carol didn't know this man at all, she called Robin and asked her advice on whom they should see, what they should do, and how Carol should follow up. Robin gave Carol some helpful tips, and the days with the honcho went reasonably well.

Two months later, Robin's boss, the man Carol had worked with, called to offer her a promotion. Later, Carol found out that Robin had played a big role in letting people know about her work, her interest in the company, and her long-term career goals. She also communicated her feelings to her immediate manager in a follow-up letter after their work trip.

Carol's relationship with Robin worked both ways. Because Robin believed in Carol and was willing to go to bat for her, Carol was extremely loyal. She volunteered to help her with special projects, went the extra mile to get information for her, and was thoroughly motivated by her intelligence and work.

When Carol was promoted to a job in New York City, she and Robin continued to work closely together. Robin is one of the main reasons that Carol was able to make a smooth start in a territory which was a real stretch for her skill level at that time.

To this day, they are still close. Robin still teaches Carol many things, and Carol has the same admiration and respect for Robin that she had at the beginning.

You can find mentors outside the company as well as inside. Carol's brother Craig, for example, has always been a mentor for her. He markets cellular phones for Motorola, and there are many similarities between his and Carol's departments. He often gives Carol advice when she is not sure how to solve a particular problem. Listening to his experiences and noticing the similarities between their two jobs gives Carol the perspective she needs, not to mention the emotional support to work through difficult situations.

Tips on choosing a mentor

1. *Find someone with experience whom you respect.*

2. *Be sensitive to his or her time.* He or she has a job to do as well.

3. *Don't just take.* Give. Find a way you can help the person do his or her job better. Otherwise, what incentive do they have to help you?

"It's important to find people you can admire." Adam Lerner, a Ph.D. student in political science at Johns Hopkins University, sums it up perfectly. "Mentors are life teachers. You learn certain things from some, other things from others. But don't hold your mentor to an unrealistic standard."

Adam brings up an important point. You can outgrow your mentor. Recognize people's shortcomings while accepting their attributes. See the human side of your heroes and role models. When someone no longer challenges you, it may be time to move on to another mentor. But don't put yourself on too high a horse; remember what got you to this stage.

Maintaining perspective

So, do you balance all these relationships at once: your peers, your manager, your mentor? It depends on your priorities; the cycle of your year (some months are busier than others), and the other relationships you have to maintain. It does take special patience to keep all parties informed, motivated, and at ease, especially when your stress level is running high. Work at it. It's most difficult in your first year, when you are just learning the job. That's when it matters the least. As your skill level and experience increase, management will reward your managerial abilities.

This chapter has covered a lot of ground, from managing your manager, your co-workers, and your mentor to handling yourself in teams and meetings. With so much going on in your first couple of years out of school, it is easy to be overwhelmed by the complexity of managing relationships. When you are under stress, it is very easy to worry about the next person. At times like this, it is important to step back and mind your own business. At the most basic level, if you do your job well and become a role model for others, you'll be valued and appreciated by others. So few people are truly exemplary. Be one of them.

Auto Focus:

Handling Success and Failure

Adversity has the effect of exciting talents which, in prosperous circumstances, would have lain dormant.   —*Horace*

The play's the thing.   —*William Shakespeare*

"I tried and failed, I tried again and again and succeeded," reads the tombstone of Gail Borden, who made his fortune in the dairy business, which he entered at the age of fifty-three. Among his memorable failures were the "terraqueous wagon," a four-wheeled vehicle designed to travel equally well on sea or land (which nearly drowned the town leaders of Galveston, Texas); a giant refrigerated building for townspeople to live in during the summer when diseases spread most quickly; and a dehydrated meat biscuit that would not spoil (though it did win a gold medal at the London Crystal Palace Exposition in 1851).

In 1856, he patented his process for making sweetened condensed milk and began to manufacture the product. He and his partners were soon bankrupt. A year later, he opened a new plant with the substantial backing of a New York banker. The rest is history. As you know, Borden is now one of the world's largest manufacturers of dairy products. Some of Borden's ideas were great; most were failures. But he wasn't about to let anything get in his way.

Over the years, people have attached different values to winning and losing. For Vince Lombardi, famous coach of the Green Bay Packers, "winning wasn't everything, it was the only thing." Others would disagree. People love to draw analogies between sports and business, and there certainly are some parallels. People who play hard tend to work hard. Gracious losers on the tennis courts tend to behave the same way in the office.

But carrying the analogy too far can lead to misconceptions and even trouble. Because, in business, every day is game day, and the end, the victory, does not always justify the means. In fact, how you handle winning and losing is more important than a given outcome. The thrill of victory and the agony of defeat can be an emotional seesaw. What counts is your ability to rise above the fray and act maturely and fairly. In the long run, how you "play," and how you conduct yourself before, during, and after the game is most important.

Success is hardly coincidental—it's a series of progressive steps toward a predetermined goal. While you are taking these steps, you should visualize not only what your next step will be but also what you'll do once you're at the top of the first flight of stairs, or, alternatively, lying at the bottom. Very, very rarely do you hop, skip, and jump to the top without pausing to hold on to the handrail. And be prepared, you will fall down. The trick is to make sure someone is there to catch you and that you fall elegantly. And when you do succeed, to make sure you haven't pushed anyone down the stairs on your way to the top.

How you will be evaluated

1. *Performance Reviews.* Performance reviews are simply that—they evaluate what you have done over the last year. It is a formal opportunity for your manager to let you know how the company views your results, compared to everyone else in similar positions. This knowledge is critical for your short- and long-term success.

In Chapter 3, we talked about goal-setting and performance objectives. Your performance evaluation will be the first time you will formally confront success or failure. Companies all have different styles, philosophies, and approaches to evaluating employee performance. Ideally, the performance evaluation is an open forum between you and your manager. Employees and managers complete a similar form on what the employee has accomplished, where he is strong, and where he needs to improve. Together, they discuss not only what happened throughout the year but also qualities and characteristics which the company values in its employees—teamwork, leadership, stress tolerance, adaptability, etc.

2. *Raises*. Sometimes your manager will give you a raise without a review. Most frequently, you will have a performance review a few weeks before you are given a salary increase. This is an ideal situation, since your performance review and the feedback you receive on how you can do your job better should not be clouded by a percentage increase in salary. Your raise may not meet your expectations. If you are upset about it, try to separate it from your performance feedback. The only way to improve on the job is to have a realistic understanding of where you are and where you have to go.

Remember, raises are given for adequate, above average, or outstanding performance. If you're not performing at the minimum requirement level, you may not be given an increase at all. If this happens, take heart. Summon the courage and the energy that are within you and do your best next year. Chances are that with improved results you'll get an increase that is fair.

At some level, all performance evaluations are based on a comparison with your fellow workers. Currently, there is a strong move toward a process called the pool review. In this system, the manager rates each employee versus the other employees and decides how much of a set sum to apportion to each worker. Under this system, it is not unheard of for a poor performer to get zero salary increase. Companies like IBM, known for their no-lay-off policy, are using this type of review to put pressure on poor performers and reward the better employees. If your company uses this system, it's especially important for you to set very specific up-front expectations and goals early in the review calendar. That way, you establish a measuring stick for everyone's performance.

At the opposite end, some companies still do not conduct formal reviews. Your review may consist of a simple statement: "You're getting a five percent increase." Even worse, at many companies you won't get a review unless you ask for it. In these cases, you have to take the initiative and ask for feedback. You won't improve unless you get a fair assessment of your strengths and weaknesses. Few people are objective enough to see things clearly without a little help from the outside. You won't succeed in changing company policy, but you can and should expect feedback on your performance.

TIPS FOR HANDLING YOUR REVIEW

1. *If you didn't ask when you were hired, find out when, where, and how you'll be evaluated.*

2. *Review yourself before you are reviewed.* If you have done a good job of keeping your manager informed of your goals, your review shouldn't come as a surprise.

3. *Don't take it personally.* Don't confuse criticism with condemnation. No one is perfect, and don't expect your manager to make you the first exception.

4. *In case of dispute, have documentation ready.* Very rarely will your review disagree with your performance, but in case it does, be prepared to answer your supervisor's questions with cold, hard facts.

For the most part, managers have to complete some type of form which will serve as the basis for a discussion. At the time, you may want to bring out the goals you set at the beginning of the year. How did you do? What more could you have done? What can you do better next year?

Here are some of the things you may be evaluated on in addition to your overall job performance:

Quality of work
Quantity of work
Planning and organization
Teamwork
Delegation
Control
Attitude
Initiative
Leadership
Adaptability
Vision
Problem-solving
Decision-making
Knowledge of the job
Knowledge of the company
Knowledge of the industry

Receiving your review

If you have already completed your "year in review" self-appraisal, analyzing all the goals you set initially (as you did in Chapter 3), then you probably have a good idea of where you stand. Since your review is usually a dialogue between you and your manager, take the time to explain where you feel your strengths and weaknesses are and what you'd like to do to improve. Your honesty and judgment will show your manager that you are mature and open to suggestions.

Keep an open mind during your review. You may not agree with the feedback. You may not agree with the whole review. Keep calm. The point of the review is to help you, not hurt you. Over time, when you develop a greater perspective, you may better understand your manager's comments, or you may always disagree—but don't show it. If you can improve performance without heeding advice you disagree with, more power to you. If not, swallow your pride, buck up, and think how you can implement the suggestions you have been given.

Follow-up after the review

After you've digested your review, think about the goals you'd like to set for next year. Discuss them with your manager and anyone else you feel should know about them.

If you'd like to discuss your progress with your manager on a monthly basis, ask him or her. Not all managers are good at giving continual feedback, and not all employees are mature enough to handle it. Do what's most helpful to allow you to improve, communicate with your manager, and grow in your job.

If it's time for more of a challenge, or if you'd like to discuss your long-term career options, this may be an appropriate time. If you have been in your job for a few years and you are making progress, upper management will probably be interested in encouraging you along the career path you find most interesting.

Handling success

Jim Click is a very successful businessman from Carol's hometown. He is near and dear to her heart because he gave her a scholarship while she was in college. She has always admired him because at a young

SAMPLE REVIEW USA COMPANY

- Prioritize **strengths** by placing a number next to each strength checked (1-strongest).
- Prioritize **development needs** by placing a number next to each need checked (1-**most** critical need).
- Provide specific job-related examples to further explain the prioritized strengths and needs.
- Complete Career Planning and Development Strategies section on reverse side.

SKILLS PROFILE

EMPLOYEE'S NAME		DATE	
Angela Meranza			
MANAGER'S NAME		COMPLETING THIS FORM AS	
Michael Kiraden		Employee ☒ Manager	

MANAGEMENT SKILLS PROFILE	STRENGTHS Possesses Rank ( ) (#)	DEVELOPMENT NEEDS Needs Rank ( ) (#)	SPECIFIC ON-THE-JOB EXAMPLES
COMMUNICATION SKILLS	✓ 4	✓	*I feel comfortable here. I believe I communicate well with others*
CREATIVITY INNOVATIVENESS			*In my current job, I haven't had a chance to prove these skills*
DECISIVENESS			
TENACITY	✓ 2		*I stick to projects, despite the difficulty. Because of my inexperience, I frequently don't know what to do!*
FUNCTIONAL SKILLS INDUSTRY KNOWLEDGE		✓ 1	
INDEPENDENCE			
INTERPERSONAL SKILLS	✓ 1		
JUDGMENT			
LEADERSHIP IMPACT			
PEOPLE MANAGEMENT SKILLS			*I haven't had a chance to prove this yet.*
PERSONAL ADAPTABILITY			
PLANNING ORGANIZING SKILLS		✓ 3	*I consider myself very organized but I have difficulty setting priorities*
PROBLEM SOLVING ANALYTICAL SKILLS		✓ 2	*Will improve with experience.*
RESULTS GOAL-ORIENTED	✓ 3		
STREET SMARTS			
BUSINESS SAVVY			
STRESS TOLERANCE	✓ 6		*I manage stress by working out*
TEAM PLAYER	✓ 5		*I try to help others as much as possible with what I've learned or what I've done*
CITIZENSHIP			

CAREER PLANNING PREPARATION

- Career interests (1–3 years)
- Type of experiences (e.g., more divisional exposure, cross-functional project assignment)
- Supervisory support of development
- Employee commitment to development

NOTES

Personal career goal → manager within 3 years
interest in doing a field assignment
take one more responsibility outside my job to learn the big picture
very committed to career and personal development

DEVELOPMENT STRATEGIES

Identify 2–3 strategies for each of the prioritized strengths and needs.

1) communication - would like to attend career development session

2) industry knowledge - continue to question others in the business re: their role, responsibilities, career paths

3) setting priorities - will continue to seek advice on this weekly

4) analytical skills - practice, practice, practice. Continue to reason through my instincts with others.

SAMPLE REVIEW USA COMPANY

- Prioritize **strengths** by placing a number next to each strength checked (1-strongest).
- Prioritize **development needs** by placing a number next to each need checked (1-**most** critical need).
- Provide specific job-related examples to further explain the prioritized strengths and needs.
- Complete Career Planning and Development Strategies section on reverse side.

SKILLS PROFILE

EMPLOYEE'S NAME: *AMANDA MORALES*   DATE:

MANAGER'S NAME: *Gilbert Guiera*   COMPLETING THIS FORM AS: Employee / Manager ✓

MANAGEMENT SKILLS PROFILE	STRENGTHS Possesses ( )	Rank (#)	DEVELOPMENT NEEDS Needs ( )	Rank (#)	SPECIFIC ON-THE-JOB EXAMPLES
COMMUNICATION SKILLS	✓	1			Good at communicating with co-workers
CREATIVITY INNOVATIVENESS			✓	3	Can develop in connection with problem solving
DECISIVENESS	✓	2			can take more time with key decisions
TENACITY	✓	1			
FUNCTIONAL SKILLS INDUSTRY KNOWLEDGE			✓	2	This will come with experience
INDEPENDENCE	✓	2			
INTERPERSONAL SKILLS					
JUDGMENT			✓	2	Again, a matter of experience and time
LEADERSHIP IMPACT			✓	2	can learn to have a stronger impact with others
PEOPLE MANAGEMENT SKILLS	✓	2			Diplomatic, but doesn't exercise authority
PERSONAL ADAPTABILITY	✓	2			
PLANNING ORGANIZING SKILLS			✓	3	can be more focused and set better priorities
PROBLEM SOLVING ANALYTICAL SKILLS	✓	2			good innate skills. can develop and sharpen
RESULTS GOAL-ORIENTED	✓	1			
STREET SMARTS	✓	1			
BUSINESS SAVVY			✓	2	
STRESS TOLERANCE			✓	2	needs to develop a game face and show emotions less
TEAM PLAYER	✓	2			
CITIZENSHIP	✓	1			

CAREER PLANNING PREPARATION

- Career interests (1–3 years)
- Type of experiences (e.g., more divisional exposure, cross-functional project assignment)
- Supervisory support of development
- Employee commitment to development

NOTES

Very good potential for the long term. Although the first year was rocky in some respects. She has a firm understanding of what she must do to meet her objectives next year. She has strong innate talent which can be refined with her diligence and determination.

DEVELOPMENT STRATEGIES

Identify 2–3 strategies for each of the prioritized strengths and needs.

Amanda would like to be a local area manager in two to three years. To achieve this, she must become stronger strategically, learning what's most important for herself and for others. She must also learn to lead and direct people to a desired outcome.

age he achieved success and yet has managed to remain humble through the years.

Success didn't come to Jim easily. As a recent graduate from Oklahoma State University, Jim did not make a single sale in his first few weeks on the job as a car salesman. He felt dejected and discouraged. He called his dad and a few other friends, who gave him advice. "Call your friends and tell them what you're doing. Maybe they'll know people who can help." "Don't quit," his dad said. "Just keep at it." Jim did keep at it. And today he has a highly successful car dealership in Arizona and California. He is also an active and influential citizen in the state of Arizona.

For many people, success is harder to deal with than failure. Surprised? It's true. If you fail, you can always pick yourself up. If you succeed, however, it may be hard to rein in your joy of accomplishment. Our advice is: When things go well, retain your humility. Don't let your head expand. If you think you're doing great and you get used to patting yourself on the back too much, your judgment won't be clear.

Success isn't a bad word

It's easy to become obsessed with success and end up self-destructing. History is filled with individuals who have done just that. That's why it is important to be comfortable with success, both personally and professionally. Personally, you should feel justified and secure about your accomplishments, without feeling overconfident. The best way to keep on track is to revisit the road you took, so you know exactly how you got where you are and to see if you can duplicate the process in another area of your job or life. Chart out the steps you took.

How long did it take? What were the key events? Who were the key players? Did you make one or two critical decisions? Perhaps you made one or two extra phone calls, looked at a problem in a different way, or simply worked harder. Whatever the cause, you need to be able to document it for yourself. Once you're comfortable with your achievement, you'll be able to achieve more and ease any doubt as to why or how you got there.

Fear of success

Why is it important to analyze your success? People often fear success. We feel guilty about winning, so we avoid it. Feel guilty about winning? Are you crazy? I love to win! If so, you are fortunate, since most people have some level of innate fear of success. Certainly we all want to succeed, but success brings more pressure to succeed and focuses more attention on the winner. You can also start to question your success. That's when you'll hear yourself answer: "Oh, it was nothing, I got lucky," or "I just happened to be in the right place at the right time."

Here's a situation that we've all experienced in one form or another. The test you took for one of your classes had exactly the questions you studied for. You didn't study everything, just the material you figured would be on the test. You ended up acing the test. You feel guilty because you know there are other people who studied harder than you did. You write off your success. Don't! Instead, consider why you picked those questions, to see if you can apply the process to another class. Get to know why you succeeded, assume it was a right move, not just luck.

TIPS FOR BECOMING PERSONALLY COMFORTABLE WITH SUCCESS

1. *Map your success.* You can do this chronologically or by task or event. If you are working on a major project, you probably charted it before you even started, and referred to your plan along the way. Surprisingly few people realize the importance of looking at the plan after you're done! This will give you a visual sense of your success and help you understand the steps that helped you get there.

2. *Highlight the obstacles.* Business is more complex than college, but even the most complicated business situations usually boil down to one or two major obstacles. It will take a series of steps on your part to determine what those obstacles are, and another series of steps to overcome them. By highlighting the obstacles on your map, you'll be in a better position to study the reasons for your success. What did you have to overcome to get where you got? Who or what was in the way? Did you knock off obstacles one at a time? Whose help did you enlist?

3. *Duplicate the process.* One of the most beautiful things about success is that it can usually be duplicated quickly and easily. That's because, as we said before, success is a series of steps. It's not one simple action; it's a compendium of actions, a process. Remember the first time you did a jigsaw puzzle? It probably took you a while to figure out that the best way to go about it was to start with the edges and work your way inward. The next time you worked on a puzzle, did you follow that strategy? We hope so. You can duplicate your successes. Don't start from scratch.

Handling success at work

Here's the tricky part of the equation: You can backtrack and become comfortable with your success personally because it involves only you and your feelings. But in order to handle success professionally, where many other people are involved, you need to start at day one—before you achieved anything.

As we have mentioned, small groups, the team approach, will become the prevalent division of labor in the nineties. This arrangement will make it increasingly difficult for you to separate your personal success or failure from that of the team. It will be all the more difficult to handle, because it runs counter to the way we've been brought up. Our seventies and eighties role models have been the "lone rangers," out on their own, making things happen: Donald Trump, Lee Iacocca, etc. It's naturally difficult for us to split the attention and share the recognition. Because you will be sharing your success with others, the importance of handling it well is magnified.

▶ *Test yourself*

A co-worker who is not as efficient as you are has just received a promotion or been praised for his work. The word around the office is that he brown-nosed his way to recognition, or he got lucky and happened to be in the right spot at the right time. The real reason for his success doesn't matter. There is a sea of jealousy out there. How would you respond?

Does this situation sound familiar? It should! It's probably what people are saying about you and your good test score. If you think people have a fear of success, you should see their fear of failure. And that is exactly what happens when someone succeeds. Everyone else automatically, and incorrectly, thinks they are failing.

But notice how our victim of success handles all this abuse. Maybe he becomes completely isolated, setting his own course and alienating his co-workers. Worse, he may start to think he is God's gift to the workplace and walk around like the biggest rat in the cheese factory. What's the cause? Part of it is probably his inability to handle personal success, but, more important, no one expected or shared his success.

1. *Involve other people.* As we have said, your success may be part of a larger successful venture. Learn to share your ideas and accomplishments early in your career. Think of yourself as a company. In order to make new products or pursue new ventures, you need to raise capital. You can do that by getting a loan or selling shares of stock, giving other people a vested interest in seeing that you do well. As you continue to perform, more and more people are interested in investing in you. Success breeds success.

Let people know what you're up to! If they know the steps that lead to your success, then they'll be more comfortable accepting it. The other reason to involve people is more obvious: they will help you. For the most part, people will flock to a good thing and further the cause. In the worst case, they'll be a sounding board for your ideas. Now, we aren't suggesting you share every living moment, only the highlights or the obstacles. And only with some people. Remember your map. It serves as your working tool for handling both personal and professional success.

2. *Communicate your wins.* This is another way of saying, "Take some credit." Occasionally, we've seen a success for which no one seems to be responsible. What a shame for you, your co-workers, and your organization. You've just scored a major victory, but you aren't sure how, when, or why. As you climb up and over each major obstacle, make sure some people know it. Document your work, either formally in a memo or informally in a file. Several people we know at work keep every single piece of paper associated with any project.

3. *Don't gloat.* If you've involved others and told them what you're doing, you'll most likely get the recognition you deserve. No one can stand a poor winner. So don't live by your successes, live by the process you took to reach it—you'll be called on to succeed again. Learn to say thank you. Eliminate the phrases "Ah, it was nothing," or "It was no big deal," from your vocabulary.

TIPS FOR HANDLING SUCCESS PROFESSIONALLY

1. *Give people a stake in your success.* Sell shares in your company (you), but retain the controlling interest. Any time there is a major decision or obstacle, let the stockholders vote.

2. *Document your wins.* Let your managers know your wins. Don't deluge them with paper, but keep them informed. Your organization may provide you with the means to do this via a monthly report or a similar document. If not, take matters into your own hands.

3. *Be gracious.* The best way to take a compliment is with a simple "Thank you." Don't search out a compliment and don't ignore it when it is offered. Most people find it as difficult to give as to receive.

Handling failure

The most important thing to remember about failure is that it happens. The most successful people in business are often those who had the biggest failures. Everyone remembers the Macintosh and the IBM PC, but does anyone remember the PC, Jr. or the Apple Lisa? How about the record or movie industry? There are literally hundreds of losers waiting for you at the $2.99 bin or lined up on the video counter. Someone made the decision to go ahead and produce that material.

The bottom line is that someone has to do something or nothing gets done. And any time you do something you have a real chance of failing. The business world is too complex to avoid an occasional failure, much more complex than school. The success of a project also depends on such factors as the economy, your co-workers, and your competition. Fortunately for you, when you start out, the stakes are much lower. You can afford to take chances, to go out on a limb.

"People who don't succeed give up too soon," says Anita Brick, who works for Decision Dynamics in Chicago. Anita, who also hosts her own talk show, called "No Matter What," says that our generation grew up on "instant everything" and, as a result, we've lost our ability to persist. "Patience and tenacity are two extremely important qualities which are seldom found in today's twenty- and thirty-something crowd. What they don't realize is that you can't succeed without failing."

Now, just because failure is part of the equation of success doesn't make it any easier to stomach. As one of our friends loves to joke when people are talking about their trials and tribulations: "What about me? What about my problems?" There are still going to be tough times, times when you question your every action. Relax. Failure happens to all of us, it's usually for the best, and there are constructive ways of dealing with it.

Limiting your losses

The most important and mature decision you can make is to limit the damage. In business, you generally don't spend time trying to bring a D grade up to a C when you can spend your time elsewhere and get an A. It isn't simply of a case of working harder; it's working smarter or elsewhere.

For example, our organization was once involved in a major publishing agreement with a software company that supplied us with software which we put into a textbook for students. Unfortunately, the product never caught on, despite Herculean efforts by both parties. Late in the process, we were given the option of continuing our agreement with the original company or making a similar arrangement with another vendor. Although we had invested enormous amounts of time, effort, and money with the original company, we switched to the other vendor. Why? Because any additional effort with the original company would yield only incremental gain. The same amount of effort put into a new venture had the potential to generate greater revenue. It's that simple: Don't throw good money after bad. Incidentally, we later returned to the original company and using what we had learned in the first relationship, succeeded with another product.

CASE IN POINT
Stan's stamina

Stan Howard left a job in New York City with Morgan Stanley to start his own real estate business in the land of the sun and waves, Hawaii. The first six months were very bleak. There was a recession in the United States, and the Japanese economy—a mainstay for his business—was also sluggish. Stan had to sell his house and move to a smaller place. There was one setback after another, but he kept plugging away, making contacts and working hard. He watched his savings dwindle before his eyes.

Finally, after many months, a break came. He met a successful Japanese real estate investor who was interested in one of his properties. The two had an instant rapport, and when the man returned to Japan, he called Stan to invite him to Tokyo. The men worked together to plan how Stan's business could grow and accommodate the Japanese client's business.

This was the big break that made months of hard work and financial worry pay off. Stan could have given up and taken another job when his savings started to dwindle, but he persisted. He now has more business than he can keep up with, and he is working on expanding his already healthy client base.

Waving the magic wand

Wouldn't you love to have a fairy godmother who would constantly tell how well you are doing and whether or not you are doing the right thing? You may have a mentor or manager who will keep you posted, but if you don't, how do you know when you are failing? Sometimes, as in our company's arrangement with the software company, you can't really tell. When you are doing something for the first time, it's hard to find a good measure. In these situations, when you have no internal experience to draw on, it's best to look outside for the yardstick. When we needed a measure for our software deal, we looked at what our competition was doing. Now, obviously, you can't compare yourself to a company, but you can look at your peers. How well are they doing? How does your situation parallel theirs?

TIPS FOR TELLING HOW WELL YOU'RE DOING

1. *Find a measure.* Most jobs have a quantitative and qualitative component: sales quotas, deadlines, production efficiency, money saved, etc. If you don't have a formal measure, find one!

2. *Find someone to compare yourself to.* Don't go comparing yourself to someone who's been in the job for twenty years. Find a co-worker with slightly more experience, someone who is where you want to be.

3. *Be realistic.* Don't expect too much too soon. Real success or failure doesn't really come for at least six months. It takes a while to learn.

4. *Ask!* Ask your boss and co-workers you respect. It's not a sign of weakness unless you get too compulsive and ask every day. But you should learn to check in periodically.

After the fall

Okay, so you've asked around, you've gone through the steps and determined you are not making the grade. People are avoiding you in the hallways; you need help, a life, a new job, a clue. Wait. Take a deep breath. Get those reins back. The first thing to remember is: Don't panic! There is no such thing as a quick fix. Take a moment to gather your thoughts, figure out what happened, and decide what to do next.

CASE IN POINT
The deaf musician

One of the greatest composers of all times, Ludwig van Beethoven, went through a very tough time early in his career. He had a major setback: by the age of thirty, he had suffered a hearing loss for which there was no cure. However, he had a very well trained "inner ear," and he could "hear" music just by looking at it on the page. His career as a pianist was over, his dreams shattered, his gainful employment as a piano teacher finished—and that was his primary way to earn money. He was discouraged and depressed.

Eventually, however, his will and inner faith prevailed. As he said, he "seized fate by the throat" and committed himself to "produce all the works that he felt the urge to write." This renewed strength and energy made it possible for him to do some of his best work, which reflects the passion and commitment in his heart. If you've ever heard his Ninth Symphony, you know the power of his determination in the depth and strength of the music.

Sometimes it's useful to recognize the trials and tribulations that people have endured throughout history. Understanding what they've gone through can be a comfort to you when the curve balls, however large or small, are hurled your way.

TIPS FOR HANDLING FAILURE

Strangely enough, there's very little difference between handling failure and success well. We've both grown the most from our failures and setbacks. In fact, at times we've thought it impossible for our character to be developed any further from those "character-building experiences"—that age-old euphemism for "when bad things happen to good people."

Kidding aside, failing is part of living. No success comes without it. When it happens, and, typically, it happens to most of us on a consistent basis, you have to summon up all your courage and your best energy to redirect yourself. Whether you've been fired from a job (estimates indicate that we will all be fired from at least one job some time in our career), laid off, or didn't get the promotion you wanted, regard your disappointment as an opportunity. What you do with the situation will determine whether you experience a temporary setback or a total, dead-in-the-water failure.

1. *Map your failures.* What went wrong and when? Was it totally within your control? Can you establish a cause-and-effect relationship? In her book, *Uncommon Genius*, Denise Sheherjian asked famous psychologist Howard Gardner how he keeps up his spirits when research fails, grants fall through, and colleagues begin to doubt him. She writes: "Howard Gardner isn't afraid to examine his mistakes. He doesn't run from them, but, instead, steps back and takes an appraising look with a cool, friendly eye, trying to isolate what went wrong and why."

Gardner, like many others, studies his failures and then uses what he learns to set new goals. "Confidence," Sheherjian concludes, "comes from success, to be sure, but it can also come from recognizing that a lot of carefully examined failures are themselves paths to success."

2. *Highlight the pitfalls.* Was it one big mistake or a series of mistakes? (This might help you determine if the failure was habitual or circumstantial.) When did the mistakes occur? Was it a structural mistake: i.e., something you did in organizing the task or work? Or was the mistake made in execution? Who else was involved? What do they think?

3. *Don't duplicate the process.* You need to build a mental data base of your successes and failures so you can call on them when you analyze similar situations.

TIPS FOR HANDLING FAILURE PROFESSIONALLY

Is there really a difference between how you handle failure at home or at work? Sure. At work, you probably wouldn't cry your eyes out or start screaming. At home, that might be just the cure. At home, you might share all the details and blame with someone who will be understanding. At work, it is best to keep your feelings to yourself and plan a new course of action.

1. *Involve others.* Involve people at the outset, not right at the end, when you are the only one who knows you're doomed. Remember the shares you sold in your success? Well, those same stockholders need to step up when things go wrong. Call on your co-workers to validate and analyze your failure.

2. *Communicate.* Letting people know how and why you lost is as important as letting them know how and why you won. It shows you are a good sport and know how to keep your perspective. We aren't suggesting that you walk through the halls sporting a banner with the words "Don't Be Like Me" on it, but you should be prepared to present a reasonable analysis of your failure to anyone who asks.

3. *Don't pout.* As we have said, everyone fails; it is a natural thing. Everyone around you, at work and at play, has been in similar situations. If you appear to have lost your confidence altogether, you'll discourage people from letting you try again.

4. *Don't get paranoid.* With your first few failures, there's a tendency to defend yourself too vigorously or to try to point the blame elsewhere. Don't fall into that trap—it's a sign of immaturity. Learn to shoulder the blame rationally, not to shy away from it or deflect it, but rather to let people know you're aware of what went wrong and know how to fix it.

There's nothing to fear but fear itself

In the end, how you handle success or failure really comes down to your level of self-confidence. Do you have the willpower to take credit for your wins and blame for your losses? Can you "keep on going on," either way?

"Stand on the high dive and look into the pool and it can be scary," says Dr. Jerald Jellison, a professor at the University of Southern California. "Jump from the pool edge first, then the low board, and you build your confidence and willingness to take risks. Break a frightening project into small steps and usually the fear vanishes."

Jellison is right. If you attack your fears head-on and develop a reasonable game plan for yourself, what you have to do becomes far less daunting. Try it the next time you undertake an ambitious or risky task.

CASE IN POINT
Missing the high note

After a successful academic career culminating in a Master's degree in music and several performance awards, Susan Demler got married, moved to Houston, and started trying to break into opera.

One of Susan's first auditions was with a very well known musician. Although Susan was confident in her abilities and talents, she was intimidated by the man's fame and the whole process of auditioning. She was also by nature self-effacing, generous, and non-competitive. "Naïve" might be a better word to describe her at that time in her career. In the competitive world of opera singing, there is a great deal of professional jealousy and backbiting. As the saying goes: "There can be only one prima donna." Because Susan was so nice, her fellow auditioners saw her as easy prey. She sang well in her audition, but, discouraged and intimidated by their behavior, she acted too nervous and inexperienced to land the part.

Looking back, Susan saw what had happened. "I let my colleagues prey on my insecurities. I was so green that I let them psych me out. If I had shut my eyes and ears to them, my audition would have been stronger and my actions with the musician would have been more powerful. My mistake was that I came off as too naïve and too lacking in confidence. I learned that if you're a nice person, people will take advantage of you if you don't assert yourself. They'll try to tell you you can't handle something when you know you can.

"If you don't listen to your own voice, you'll let people convince you of all kinds of things. Stand your ground and take the plunge. Even if you don't think you're up for a job, you should go for it anyway. Chances are, you are just as qualified, if not more qualified, than the next person. Be confident. It's a huge part of approaching anything you do in life."

This lesson was to serve Susan well, especially when she heard later that the director preferred her voice, but didn't choose her because she was "like a deer in the headlights." Now she's a part-time opera singer and part-time publicist on her way to a successful singing career. "I'll never, never underestimate myself again," she says.

A final word

Susan Demler was able to turn her failure into a positive experience. Handling success and failure in the workplace is one of the most difficult and important lessons to learn. Your response to success and failure will push the limits of your personality and leave you feeling and acting in ways you never thought were possible. During times like these, it's a good idea to bounce your feelings off a close friend or relative, someone totally impartial to the situation. Walk through your map with an innocent and unbiased bystander. And most of all, don't make winning or losing more personal than it needs to be. In the end, how you play is more important.

Finally, we want to remind you that, despite your best efforts, personal success and failure will naturally affect how you feel on the job. If your boyfriend or girlfriend breaks up with you or the deal falls through on your new apartment, you may not feel like setting the world on fire at work. During these times, it is important to draw the fine line between work and your personal life. The following words from Winston Churchill sum it up best: "Success is the ability to go from one failure to another with no loss of enthusiasm."

The Wide-Angle Lens:

Understanding the Qualities

of Success

*Where I was born and where and how I lived is unimportant. It is what I have done
with where I have been that should be of interest.* —Georgia O'Keeffe

*If one has a talent and cannot use it, he has failed. If he has a talent and uses only
half of it, he has partly failed. If he has a talent and somehow learns to use the whole
of it, he has gloriously succeeded, and won a satisfaction and a triumph few men ever
know.* —Thomas Wolfe

One never notices what has been done; one can only see what remains to be done.
—Marie Curie

Whom do you think of when you think of successful people? Why do
you consider them successful? Use the space below to write down who
they are and the qualities that you think have made them successful.
Don't write down only famous people, since you may know only about
their achievements, not the process by which they accomplished their
goals. Try to think of someone who's not famous but whom you know
personally.

SUCCESSFUL PEOPLE: QUALITIES:

1. _____   _____

                                      _____

                                      _____

2. _____   _____

                                      _____

                                      _____

3. _____   _____

                                      _____

                                      _____

4. _____   _____

                                      _____

                                      _____

5. _____   _____

      _____

      _____

Now take a look at your list. Do these people share any particular strengths? Most likely, you have a cross section of people. There's probably some overlap in their attributes, but a great diversity as well.

Success in the workplace comes in a variety of shapes and sizes, from Dr. Ruth Westheimer to San Antonio Spurs' star, David Robinson. There is no one absolute formula. It may seem that being successful has more to do with luck than with any one thing a person can control. Certainly, luck comes into play, but don't be fooled. Most successful people followed a long and arduous path that they cut for themselves, using their individual skills and talents. As an old saying goes: "The harder I work, the luckier I become."

CASE IN POINT
The first black justice

Thurgood Marshall is a trailblazer in a number of ways. He exemplifies many qualities of success but will be remembered most notably for being the first black Supreme Court Justice, appointed in 1967 by President Lyndon Johnson.

Originally from Baltimore, Maryland, Marshall graduated cum laude from Lincoln University in 1930. He had planned to be a dentist but changed his mind and started law school at Howard University, paying for his education by waiting on tables. At the time, he was not admitted to the University of Maryland Law School because of his skin color.

After graduating from law school in 1933, he practiced law in Baltimore and was married. Because he specialized in poor clients, he became known as the "little man's lawyer." On the basis of his track record, he became special counsel for the NAACP and won a famous case which resulted in the admission of blacks to the University of Texas Law School. Later in his career, he was known as "Mr. Civil Rights": he argued cases nationwide which paved the way for a number of firsts for blacks: voting rights, the outlawing of segregation on buses, and the abolition of the legal basis for segregation in public schools.

In 1961, Marshall was appointed judge to the Second Court of Appeals by President John F. Kennedy. A few years later, President Lyndon Johnson appointed him Solicitor General and then in 1967 nominated him for Associate Justice to the United States Supreme Court. Marshall, who retired from the Supreme Court in 1991, says: "My commitments have always been to justice for all people, regardless of race, creed or color."

Understanding diversity

Marshall became a Supreme Court Justice through dedication and determination. David Souter, one of President George Bush's appointees, was nominated and appointed primarily on the basis of his legal mind and his written court decisions. Clarence Thomas, in a controversial nomination, relied on charisma and tenaciousness to win his appointment. Of course, all three men had to be good lawyers and judges, but each has distinguishing characteristics beyond the fundamentals.

Have you ever been baffled by how people can be so different but hold the same job? They seem at odds stylistically and you wonder how such opposite approaches can produce quality results. Without people's different styles, outlooks, and attitudes, the world of work would be a boring, uninspiring place to spend the majority of your time. The more you are exposed to different people and their abilities, the more you stretch and grow. Think how oppressive it would be to work all day with people who are just like you.

As you read through the following pages, remember that there is no one single profile of success. There are some common qualities among successful people that you can emulate—drive, endurance, resilience—and other, more innate ones, like creativity. The trick is to develop and maximize your innate abilities and improve the skills you have.

Fortunately, most organizations realize this and are able to accommodate people's natural talents. As you work to become a successful company person, remember that it takes time. Don't try to change too many things about yourself at one time, or you may become frustrated or discouraged. In seeking to be everything to everyone, you might overlook what is most special about you. Just be aware that, over time, these may be traits you'd like to develop because they will help you, whatever direction your career might take.

The basic characteristics of success

Functional excellence

Nearly everyone would agree with Alisha Whitacre, director of management and organizational development at Colgate-Palmolive, when she says: "Functional excellence is still number-one." "You don't have to campaign for promotions," adds Don Pishney, general partner for Ernst & Young. "Your focus should be doing a good job."

Becoming skilled at your job is not an option. It's something you must do. "You have to do a good job every day," says Tony Ponturo, director of media and advertising for Anheuser Busch. "You have to have the attitude that you owe the company, not vice versa." Nothing takes the place of doing your job well or of good honest hard work.

Determination and tenacity

Carol's dad, John Carter, grew up during the Great Depression. He had one brother who died at the age of twelve, so he was an only child after that. During the Depression, his parents lost their business—Carter's Hardware store in Iowa. John was a college student at the time, but he helped his parents get back on solid financial ground. He built a miniature golf course and strung Christmas lights in the trees so that people could play at night. The proceeds from this small venture helped John's parents pay off their debts. At school he had several jobs—as an usher at a movie theater and as a waiter and soda-fountain ice-cream scooper. He worked seventy hours a week and graduated from college after five years at the University of Nebraska, Lincoln.

In their book *Entrepreneurs*, Joseph and Suzy Fucini discuss Clyde Cessna, who witnessed his first air show in 1911 and knew immediately that he wanted to fly. The thirty-one-year-old car salesman assembled his own monoplane, and never bothered to take flying lessons. He crashed fourteen times, suffering an assortment of broken bones, before safely completing his first flight! Cessna's determination and tenacity may have outweighed his common sense, but in 1925 he founded the

Travel Air Manufacturing Company with two other aviation pioneers and left two years later to form his own company, Cessna Aircraft.

What John Carter, Clyde Cessna, and most successful people share is persistence, a willingness to set a goal and follow through until it is reached. Denise Bedoin, who is a manager at CPM, Inc., a media company in Chicago, agrees. "You must have a commitment to excellence. To make good things happen, you have to have a mental and physical toughness to see things through, no matter how great the obstacles may be." Denise has moved up within her company because she is passionate about her job, she has a lot of energy and ideas to bring to others at work, and she has never stopped paying her dues. "My long hours and measured outcomes have proven my long-term capabilities to my managers," Denise says.

"Always have a positive attitude. Good things happen to good people. Success breeds success. If you are energetic and you believe in your work, you will make things happen. Be flexible and keep an open mind. Don't be afraid to admit that you don't have all the answers," says Denise.

A take-charge attitude

H. Ross Perot knew there was a groundswell of support for his candidacy for President. He went out and set up a national phone system to begin accepting and processing the thousands of calls from supporters he received each day. This was a typical act for someone who, as a new IBM sales representative, exceeded his yearly quota the very first month he had the job. Later, he went on to build one of the largest personal fortunes of the twentieth century—from scratch. All successful people take charge of themselves and their situation.

"High achievers exhibit motivation," says Olivia Carol, principal of a large metropolitan high school. "There's an air of success on projects assigned to them."

Richard Stagg, a partner in the law firm O'Connor and Cavanaugh, says: "Show initiative. You won't get far coming in and just doing your job every day."

Judy Zerafa, author of *Go For It!*, a self-help book for high school students, started her own business a few years ago. Since then, she has been interviewed by four hundred newspapers and she has given hundreds of talks to junior high and high school students. "Initially, my business was just me," says Judy. "I was the general manager, the accountant, the publicity person, and the main speaker. I had to peak every minute of every day."

Judy, whose business has grown over the last few years, now has two vice presidents who carry out different aspects of the business. But Judy isn't just a business person. She is a wife, a mom, and a grandmother. She has her entire life under control.

Irving Diamond, owner of Buy-Wize, a retail business, says: "To be successful, you must have a sense of responsibility, dependability, promptness, and loyalty, but above all you must have the initiative to accept responsibility. You're not just doing time on a job."

Successful people get more done

Thomas Alva Edison invented the record player, the light bulb, and the hearing aid. In one year, while working full-time in a patent office, Albert Einstein published three major theoretical explications, including the theory of relativity. Frank Lloyd Wright left a trail of buildings across the United States and the world. The list could go on, but the message is the same: Successful people accomplish more.

Does this mean you have to work fourteen-hour days to get ahead or be noticed? No! We all know that one person in our office who works 9 to 5 and yet has an uncanny knack for making things happen. Such people are priority-driven and have a finely developed sense of timing. They know not only what to do but when to do it. They're the "work-smart" part of the adage: "Don't work hard, work smart."

Some of you will find that you need to work long hours initially to get the work done. That's fine. That's how we started. We were willing to invest a lot of time in work. But as we gained more experience and responsibility, we realized that the large percentage of "critical" work —work that involved other people—could be done only during normal business hours.

We both happen to be morning people, so we came into the office at 7:15 for two years. In the hour before anyone else was in the building, we had time to think through the day, analyze what was most important, and get the toughest thinking jobs out of the way. Once the day gets going, it has its own rhythm. It's harder then to concentrate and make the right choices.

For the nocturnal set, this "critical thinking time" occurs between five and six or six and seven in the evening. By that time we are ready to turn off our brains. Filing and returning phone calls are the main activities for us at the end of the day. Are you a morning person or a night person?

1. *Prioritize.*

2. *Reward yourself.* It can be something as stupid as getting a candy bar from the candy machine or moving from a mundane task to a fun task.

3. *Mix good times with bad.* Don't lump together undesirable activities such as sorting your in-box or filing.

4. *Know how you work.* Do you get more done in the morning or the afternoon? At home or at work?

Quality and quantity

"I want it done right, and I want it done now." The flip side to getting more done is getting it done right; sloppy work will count against you. Your strategy for every assignment will involve balancing the quality and quantity necessary to be successful.

1. *Balance timing and quality.* Does this task need to be perfect? For example, if you're closing the financial records at the end of the year, you better get them right. If you're starting as a sales rep in a new territory at the busiest time of year, you better concern yourself with keeping up! (Nonetheless, even at the busiest times, you need to keep good records.)

2. *Double-check your work or have others do so.*

3. *Check your instincts.* On really important tasks, learn to focus on achieving quality. What would it take to make your project perfect? Even if you don't achieve perfection (and you probably won't), at least you'll know what you're striving for.

The next tier of success

Okay, so these common threads are the basics. What are the uncommon qualities that separate the great from the merely good? These skills may take time to develop but are essential to the success of many of the people we interviewed. These are the rare qualities that will make you stand out from the crowd and rise above your peers.

Successful people communicate well

We've talked a lot in this book about communicating—with your boss, your co-workers, and yourself. Communicating effectively is a skill that develops with time and especially experience. Don't confuse communication with charisma. Some people, like Martin Luther King, Jr., and Jesse Jackson, have both characteristics, but in its purest form, communicating well means getting people to believe what you are saying. You have to exude confidence in your ideas and opinions so that you can persuade others to follow your lead. This may not be so critical in your first job, but it will be important in the long haul.

CASE IN POINT
Lasting footprints

Billy Scholl, an Indiana farm boy, went to Chicago at age sixteen to become a cobbler-salesman. He embarked on a self-appointed mission to become "the foot doctor to the world" and attended medical school while working in a shoe store at night. He believed that a knowledge of foot care was essential to selling his products. He was colorful and outspoken and wrote several books on the subject. He promoted foot care in frequent interviews with the press. He sponsored a national Cinderella contest and women across the country left their footprint in their local shoe store on a Pedograph. He sponsored a series of walking marathons and crowds would wait outside the stores when the latest results were due to be posted. Billy Scholl's communication strategies allowed him to achieve success quickly, compared to most self-made businessmen. When he was twenty-five, his company became international, with the opening of a store in Canada, and at twenty-seven he expanded to London.

TIPS FOR COMMUNICATING SUCCESSFULLY

1. *Listen.* Consider your audience. Who are they? What do they want to hear? What do they need to hear? What are their characteristics? Don't open your mouth until their mouths close! Learn to spend time thinking about what they are saying, instead of thinking about what you want to say.

2. *Pick the appropriate medium.* How and when should you communicate? Should you write a memo or simply mention your idea to your colleagues? Who would hear and when? Should it be an informal discussion or a formal meeting? You may think it a casual point, but your timing and method of delivery are critical to your peers' evaluation and acceptance of your message.

3. *Be clear, be yourself, and be honest.* Use simple, honest language, but don't be impersonal or bland. If you have a certain style and it seems to be working, why send out different signals by speaking or writing in a markedly different way from the way you normally conduct yourself? Remember, what you say and what you do are inextricably linked.

One marketing manager in our organization spoke very differently in front of the department than she did to us individually. It was almost as if her evil twin had locked her in her office and come out to the meeting in her stead. We naturally came to distrust not only what she said to us in meetings, but also anything she said one-on-one.

4. *Deliver on your word.* What you say and promise to do becomes gospel. To win the loyalty of others, you must carry through on your commitments. If you really want to stand out, do more than you promise to do. People will be pleasantly surprised.

Successful people take risks

"A turtle never gets ahead without sticking out its neck." That says it all. Look for creative solutions to age-old problems or find ways to increase the capacity of your job. You need to be innovative. Maintaining the status quo is a certain dead end.

John Stern, executive vice president of Sony Corporation, values a "pro-active approach to business issues and a willingness to take risks in an entrepreneurial environment." He looks for "someone who can and wants to make things happen." Successful people who go out on a limb with a good idea have the ability to take their job and their company in new and different directions. That's crucial to the company's growth and it's what the competitive edge is all about.

Yet risk-taking at the individual level is not always easy. It's something that most managers have to work hard at encouraging their employees to do. It takes courage, guts, and fortitude. It also takes a degree of comfort with failure. Many risks don't work out. That's okay. Managers and companies realize that. But when the risks are worth it, and when they work out, they can make you stand out among your peers, help you garner company recognition at all levels, and give you a great degree of personal satisfaction.

TIPS FOR BECOMING BETTER AT RISK-TAKING

1. *Take personal risks.* One of the best ways to become comfortable taking risks on the job is to take some risks in your personal life. What have you always wanted to do but have been too afraid to try? Whether it is skydiving, deep-sea diving, learning a foreign language, or asking you next-door neighbor for a date, get used to going after things. If you fail, try something else (unless you tried skydiving!). Over time, you'll develop your confidence and you'll find that taking on challenges at work becomes easier.

2. *Learn to speak up.* Sometimes risk-taking is personal, but more often it involves more than just you. Frequently, you have to communicate what you're planning to do and convince others of the validity of your actions. Winning their confidence at the outset is not essential, but it may make the going a little easier. You can encourage others to take risks, too. By communicating your ideas, and helping others to think through their own plans, you can get the support you need and minimize your risk. Since all risks require a solid dose of good judgment —an awareness of the pitfalls and a plan for potential failure—getting the opinion of others can help you get the alternative perspective you need before you leap.

3. *Plan for failure.* All risks have a chance of not working out. That's why they are risks. If you think through all possible aspects of what can go wrong, and you anticipate how you'll deal with the potential failure, then you won't be caught short. If the downside outweighs the upside by too much, then you may want to reconsider. Maybe you'll change your plans and adjust the risk level. Whatever the risk level, be realistic about all possible outcomes and how you'll deal with each.

Think creatively

At first glance, creativity is the most colorful, memorable, and exciting trait you can develop. It is also the most frustrating, because it seems so difficult to nurture.

How can you become creative? You may never be a Walt Disney, or even an advertising writer, but you can learn to use your imagination. The following techniques can help you solve complex business problems and challenges.

1. *Learn to brainstorm.* School tends to reinforce rigid thinking. We take multiple-choice tests, which reinforce that there are only right and wrong answers. In business, it is quite different. There can be dozens of ways to solve a problem. You have to be able to come up with different angles—however outrageous—and decide which makes the most sense, given other factors, such as timing, the people involved, the complexity or implementation, etc.

Brainstorming—the art of considering numerous possibilities, from the silly to the practical—allows people to see different angles and approaches to a situation. Get in the habit of making brainstorming lists. When thinking of a way to solve a problem, take a blank piece of paper and write down absolutely everything that comes to mind, regardless of how stupid it looks or sounds. Leave your list for a few minutes and come back to it and try to make sense out of what you have written. Keep at it; brainstorming will get better as you practice opening your mind. Brainstorming is a way of keeping your mind open to the possibilities—it's a way of thinking.

▸ *Test yourself*

In a freak turn of events, your organization has decided to let its employees decide who will be its next president. Anyone can run, anyone can vote, anyone can be elected. What would your campaign slogan be? What would your platform be?

2. *Think through ideas with others.* Once you get in the habit of brainstorming, learn to be comfortable discussing your ideas with other people. Encourage them to open their minds, to develop their own ideas, and to help you criticize and develop yours. This is an enjoyable part of teamwork and, most important, it yields the best ideas.

Bebe Johnson is in the home-furnishings business. She meets with clients to determine what they want and then she thinks through her ideas with her colleague, Marilyn. "Together we come up with the best approach," Bebe says. "My instincts plus Marilyn's good ideas provide the best plan. It works well. We have a high rate of repeat customers and referrals."

3. *Look for the possibilities.* Learn to open your mind so that you see situations in terms of what they can become, not what they are at first glance. To take an organization or your job in new and different directions, you have to come up with specific ways of improving it. Don't be afraid to come up with fresh ideas. They will be welcome, regardless of the sector you are in.

If you've always been more of a cynic than an optimist, strike a balance. Retain your pragmatism, but let your mind wander and dream so that you can have the benefit of both perspectives. Starting with a big dream or ambitious vision will allow you to work your way backward to the mechanics of how, in practical terms, you can bring it all about.

4. *Make connections.* Creative people are good at seeing patterns in seemingly unrelated things. They perceive both similarities and differences and frequently come up with ingenious ways of capitalizing on a trend, a set of circumstances, or an existing need. This is how almost every invention came to be.

CASE IN POINT
The not-so La-Z-Boy

Jack Naughton was a La-Z-Boy recliner salesman during the Depression. Although he didn't have a college education, he was well trained in sales from his first job peddling Fuller Brushes door-to-door. He worked hard, and he kept his mind and his imagination active. One day, after visiting the dentist, he came up with the idea for a new chair—one that reclined like a La-Z-Boy but would be more comfortable for both patients and doctors than the upright chairs which were used at the time. Jack patented his idea in 1939, went international eight years later, and will be forever credited with inventing the reclining dental chair.

We don't know about you, but we'll probably never have an idea that creative in our lives. What we can do, however, and what anyone can learn, is to see patterns and connections on the job every day. You can get good ideas from learning what people do in other departments. You can also get great ideas from your competitors and from people in other industries. When you are impressed with interesting things which others have set in motion, ask yourself: How might this apply in my job, in my department, or in my company?

Interpersonal skills

"Interact with others in a constructive way," advises Henry Koffler, former president of the University of Arizona. Koffler came to the United States from Vienna speaking only broken English, and he worked hard to become a full professor by age thirty. "I understood how to relate to different types of people. This helped with my teachers and students and later it helped me to successfully manage groups of people when I became president."

Perhaps Koffler had a more acute sense of people since he immigrated to this country from Europe. As competition in world markets and in America grows, the products and services we need to provide become increasingly complex. We are all going to have to work hard to develop the ability to deal with people at home and abroad. Two hundred years ago Eli Whitney could invent a cotton gin that spawned an entire textile industry. Today the input of hundreds of people is required for any new product. The new superhero is the person who brings together a group's skills and maximizes the individual talents of the people involved.

"You've got to be able to relate to other people, to understand their priorities," states Tom Kilroy, director of Midwest sales for Hagger. Mel Zuckerman, founder and CEO of Canyon Ranch Resort, agrees. "The single most important quality for success is empathy. I always look for a spark behind the eyes that shows the person is thinking about the whole and not the self."

▶ *Test yourself*

Write down the full names of the many people you interact with on a daily basis. Now, how many of these do you feel you know well enough to ask for a small favor, say a ride to pick up your car, or to cover your desk for a few minutes? If the number is small, you need to expand the breadth of your relationships. If it is large, you're okay.

Now look at your list again. With how many of the people do you feel you could share a new idea about work? Is the number bigger or smaller than the number you could ask for a simple favor?

Develop a broad vision

Hindsight is 20/20, or so the saying goes. Some successful people never have to say it; they are the ones who had the long-term vision to commit to seemingly fruitless ventures. Bill Gates of Microsoft, Steven Jobs, formerly of Apple, and Philippe Kahn of Borland all had the foresight to recognize the tremendous future of the personal computer and built huge companies. Henry Ford saw a better way to build cars and revolutionized American business. At some point, probably later in your career, you will want to work to attain such a vision. For now, looking just around the corner is probably enough.

"Keep a clear vision of what you are going for," says Tom Jackson, the author of several career-tips books, including *Guerrilla Tactics in the Job Market*. "If you can always think two or three steps ahead, then you can anticipate situations and determine the best course of action. This vision," Tom says, "is what gives you the motivation to move forward."

Developing a broad vision is the most difficult characteristic of success to learn. Ultimately, it may be the most important. It's very rare that a new employee can have a "vision" for anyone other than himself, and it's even rarer that people believe him. He simply hasn't been around long enough. Unless you are hired as an analyst or a consultant and part of your job requirement is to have foresight about the industry, then you should try to develop your vision in small doses.

What do we mean by "broad vision"? In short, we mean the ability to prioritize on a personal, departmental, company-wide, or even market- or industry-wide basis. People with broad vision can successfully get their jobs done, as well as effect radical positive change in their companies. They see a big picture.

For example, one of Carol's greatest achievements at Prentice Hall was the negotiation and implementation of a cooperative venture with *The New York Times*. She identified a problem in the market: textbooks became out-of-date very quickly and lost business to more up-to-date competitors. She came up with the idea of providing students with a free update to their books, consisting of a series of hot-topics articles reprinted from *The New York Times*. Prentice Hall's competitive advantage increased significantly.

Still, Carol didn't figure this out her first year on the job. In fact, it took several years and several promotions before she was in a position to consider and negotiate such a large venture. But the basis for her vision came from seeing beyond her everyday job into the competitive markets of the publishing industry.

CASE IN POINT
A walking vision

The Rockport Shoe Company had a vision of a shoe which was both a dress shoe and a comfortable shoe to wear. Most men's shoes are anything but comfortable, so one of their employees, Bruce Katz, came up with an idea: a shoe with a rubber sole which looked like a dress shoe on the top. This shoe, he imagined, would be so comfortable that you could run in it. And run he did. He ran with the idea, marketed it well, and the shoe sold. To prove the point, Bruce Katz wore the Rockport shoes in the New York City Marathon. "As I said, they are as comfortable as running shoes" became the company's watchword. Today, the Rockport

Shoe Company is one of the largest men's shoe manufacturers in the world.

Putting it all together: becoming a leader

Leaders are those unique individuals who not only have managed to master their situations but somehow have managed to inspire others to manage theirs. We should all strive to be leaders in our own ways, but bear in mind that it is okay not to be a leader. By definition, very, very few people can be.

"Leadership can't be taught," says Jack Aiello, vice president of marketing operations for Tandy Corporation. "It must be learned by experience. Leadership is an art, not a science," says Jack, who believes that employees can develop their leadership skills by volunteering to run meetings, taking on additional responsibility, and stepping in to help other people out.

Lisa Hamilton, the operations manager of three hundred people at Super Shuttle, concurs. "Get things done ahead of time. Keep learning more aspects of the job. If you show you can handle more by already mastering what is in and out of your job description, you'll make a big statement." That's initiative and the leadership necessary to move things ahead.

"Leaders know how to turn things around," says Tom Jackson. He should know. He landed a major contract with his small staff of four by proposing an ambitious plan to help the client company. "I got a $900,000 contract which was agreed to on the back of an envelope," says Tom, who hadn't expected to be paid even half that amount. His ideas showed initiative and vision, and included the realistic steps to bring about change. The company decision-makers placed more stock in Tom than in the bigger agencies with fancy track records. He made the difference.

The best way to become a leader is by example. For you, just starting out, that means becoming proficient in the basics of your job: how much you get done, how good it is, how you deal with people—all the things we've talked about so far. If you master these challenges and move on to develop some of the qualities discussed in this chapter, you'll be on the right track to becoming a leader.

If, for whatever reason, you feel you don't have some of these qualities right now, don't worry. Just know that you can learn almost any of these things if you really want to. Your determination and ability to be disciplined about achieving goals will be the greatest determinants of your long-term success.

Paint Your Own Picture:

Decisions about Your Future

"Would you tell me, please, which way I ought to go from here?"
"That depends a good deal on where you want to get to," said the Cat.
"I don't much care where—" said Alice
"Then it doesn't matter which way you go," said the Cat.   *—Alice in Wonderland*

This time, like all times, is a very good one, if you know what to do with it.
—Ralph Waldo Emerson

Happy, motivated, mobile, and rewarded

Randy Ringer was an economics major in college. He received his master's degree in creative writing and had several articles published in well-known magazines. Randy wanted to get a steady job and work on his first novel in his spare time.

His first job was as a research analyst for a national advertising agency. It wasn't the writing job he had dreamed of, but it was a decent place to start. And though his boss sent him, "the writing expert," to a class in "business writing," he took it in good stride because he knew his job was just a stepping-stone position.

After being an analyst for a year, Randy landed the first of many promotions which would ultimately lead to his current position as vice president at another, larger advertising agency in New York, J. Walter Thompson.

What about fiction writing—his passion, his dream? In between it all, he's managed to keep the dream alive. He's had several stories published and is close to seeing his first novel in print.

If you are like Randy, your first job may be a compromise. Let's face it, times are tough and jobs are hard to come by, no matter who you are. So if you started with a job that you feel was beneath your experience or potential, then it may be time to start looking around. As long as you have made the most of the opportunity, no matter what the opportunity might be, you will be well prepared for the next step. Many people who are now running companies began their careers in the mailroom, as secretaries, or as delivery people.

Regardless of where you start, make the most of your position! Once you maximize your position, at some point it will be time to move on, whether it's to another opportunity within your organization or to another industry or a new environment. There are different theories as to when it's time seriously to consider the next move. We believe it is time to consider a move up or out after you have met two basic criteria:

1) You're bored! You know your current job cold and aren't learning anything new.

2) You have demonstrated excellence in your current position. Knowing your job cold and doing it cold are two different things. You need to be able to point to tangible accomplishments.

Note: If you are altogether unhappy, miserable, and can't bear the thought of getting out of bed to go to your job only to be harassed by an abusive boss, we recommend looking around. Many people stay in unhappy situations because they are afraid of change. You only live once.

Weigh your situation and the work environment very carefully. Waiting in a boring or non-challenging job is better than waiting in an unemployment line. Usually it is safer to look for a new opportunity while you are gainfully employed. If you are bored, find another outlet for creativity, on or off the job.

From fast track to relay race

As we've mentioned, organizations are changing the way they do business on almost every level: from how they structure themselves to how they handle technology and day-to-day business. These changes will affect the way they pay, motivate, and reward their employees.

The facts are simple. The baby-boom generation is becoming the gray wave. This graying will spell opportunity for people in our age bracket as companies have fewer and fewer people to choose from. But organizations are also placing a new emphasis on efficiency, particularly in how resources and outcomes are linked. As a consequence, they are "flattening," becoming less hierarchical, with more line people and fewer upper managers. And they are also much more capable of and willing to shift resources today than they were ten years ago—whether it is to start a new venture or to close or open divisions.

What does this mean for you? In general, there will be more non-traditional opportunities for the average employee. There will be less competition for promotions, but, overall, fewer promotional positions. The traditional fast track that our parents may have run on is being replaced with a relay race of well-paying jobs that carry more responsibility. Successful employees will be paid for performance but must be flexible enough to duplicate their success in a wider range of job responsibilities. In short, the nineties workplace will reward people who develop good, broad-based skills and pick their opportunities carefully.

Career possibilities

What are the possibilities and how should you consider them?

There are four main scenarios to consider:

1. A promotion or new assignment within your company
2. A job in your industry with another firm
3. A new industry
4. Other alternatives: school, time off, etc.

CASE IN POINT
Back to the future with Gary—thinking through the options

About four years ago, Gary had to make a difficult decision. He had been with Prentice Hall for three years and had just been promoted to an important position, managing two people and running the marketing on Prentice Hall's most important textbook. Three months into his new position, he received a very attractive job offer from an up-and-coming software company. More important, the offer came from an individual at the company whom he respected greatly. The job was fantastic. It offered potentially much more money, the company was booming, and the skills he had learned at Prentice Hall were readily transferable. The company was located in California, where he and his wife grew up and went to school and all of his family lived.

More money, closer to home, good company . . . It seemed an easy decision, but at second glance it really wasn't. He had just been promoted to the challenge of his career—launching a new product in the biggest market in the industry. He had new management responsibilities at Prentice Hall. What's more, even though his family lived out West, most of his friends were in the New York area. It was a confusing decision, one that eventually came down to a virtual mental coin toss. After two weeks of careful deliberation, he opted for California and the new job.

Nine months later, he was back at Prentice Hall.

What happened? It wasn't the job. It was all it had been cracked up to be. He made appreciably more money, the work environment was much less stressful, and he got to attend a myriad of exciting family reunions with Uncle Andy and Aunt Mildred. But something was missing. He had made a mistake in his initial consideration.

Gary had failed to consider how important the challenge of the job was to his happiness. The new position was a challenge for a while, but he wasn't managing people and his department wasn't in the limelight. There was also little room for advancement. Finally, although his wife liked being in California, she missed the excitement of her New York City magazine job.

What's to be learned from this story? Don't take a new job? Don't trade money for responsibility? Take your significant other into full consideration? (You better!) There are no easy answers, but Gary did learn a few things: If you are good, you will always have plenty of options. When it comes time to consider something else, do just that, consider it. Ask yourself what it is that makes you really happy.

Being happy has more to do with your philosophy in life—what you plan to accomplish in the long, long term and whom you want to accomplish it with—than with a particular job at a particular moment. The real trick is getting the two to merge: managing your career so that your job helps you reach the goals in your personal life.

On another level, you have to consider your obligations in a particular position. Gary left Prentice Hall at a critical time—in November, instead of in the summer. He was very fortunate in being allowed to come back. The door isn't always open. You must carefully weigh the obligation you have made to others and figure out whether your opportunity outweighs the commitment you've made to someone else. Always ask the question: Would you want someone else to treat you similarly?

Scenario 1. Getting a promotion

What you need to get the job

1. *Track record.* What you've done in your current position

The single most important criterion is how well you do your current job. Don't confuse your record with how hard you work or how many people admire you. One of the biggest questions you might be facing is: How do I know how good I am? Usually, objective measures exist: a quota, monthly reviews, etc. If not, you should ask! If your boss won't tell you, then you will probably have a problem: either she or he is weak or he or she thinks you are. If you can't get any feedback from your supervisor, ask his or her superior or your co-workers. Not knowing how well you are doing is very frustrating.

2. *Talents and abilities.* What you do well naturally, and how it fits in with what the position demands

Today, people who can adapt to "fit the job" are getting promoted as readily as super-achievers. Your ability to bring a presence and personality to a position is often more important than how many hours a day you work.

"Self-confidence based on experience and a willingness to rely on the talents of others are the most important qualities for promotion," says Michael Keeshan, president of Saatchi & Saatchi. "Being selfish instead of selfless will produce failure. The organization provides resources in the talents of the people around you. If you take advantage of those resources, you will ensure your success.

"Strive for a moment of brilliance," says Keeshan, who has been president for fourteen years. "Everyone needs a historic moment. One should be able to say that you made X contribution on X day and that it was memorable and important." Keeshan ought to know about people who made a difference. Captain Kangaroo, the inspiration for many children for years, is his dad.

3. *Potential.* How will you contribute to the company's future?

In general, promotions aren't given unless the organization believes you can grow with it.

4. *Extra credit.* The first step to promotion is to take on more than is normally required. If you understand your position, it's time to take things up a notch, to take on, as you may have done in elementary school, that "extra-credit assignment." Taking on a little more than is required is a good idea. No one gets too far just by doing an okay job at what they are supposed to do.

The trick is figuring out where to focus your effort. By now (if you've been doing your homework), you have all the resources in hand: a mentor, an understanding of the organization and its people. All you need to do is put everything together.

5. *Picking your target.* If you plan to take on the task of becoming an expert, you must do so in an area that is important to the organization. If you work for McDonald's and you want to make a difference, you'd better be sure you're spending your time learning about hamburgers. But if part of McDonald's strategic plan is to develop pizza and few people know anything about it, you might be better served by specializing in pizza. In simple terms, put yourself with the company's winners or where they want to win.

It is important to make sure any target is somehow connected to your current job. If you take on something alien, like pizza when you are working in the hamburger division, you will cause strife with your fellow workers. You'll start to hear things like "What's wrong, don't you have enough to do already?" or "You can't possibly be doing that good a job on what you are supposed to do." No one can criticize you too harshly for expanding the boundaries of your current job, but they are justified if you aren't carrying your fair share.

The plan

Once you choose an area in which to concentrate your efforts, set some goals to guide you:

1. *Have an attainable objective and take ownership.* It won't do any good to say to yourself, "Gosh, I'd like to get involved in that." You need to be specific and take ownership over a task no matter how small. People base trust on past performance. If you take on something small and complete it, you'll gradually win more and more assignments. Test your plan on a few colleagues and superiors (you may need their approval beforehand). This will strengthen your position, give others a chance to participate, and prevent you from wasting time on something that has no value to the organization.

Since organizations and environments change rapidly, we think it is a good idea for you to start with something you can get done quickly and with quality. This way, you will build confidence faster and will be ready to take on more. You can always be added to a long-term project after completing a short-term one.

2. *Develop a list of resources.* Who and what is going to help you get this done? Refer back to the organizational chart and your flow chart. Who will be the key people you will need on your side? Can your mentor help you? Is this a way to develop a new mentor? What data do you need?

3. *Have a list of things to get done.* What steps need to be taken and when? Dr. Paul Mayo agrees: "Know whether you have sufficient time and energy from within your current position."

4. *Document your work.* If you have taken the time to involve others and if your goal is important, be sure to keep people informed along the way. You need their input throughout the process, not just at the beginning and at the end.

CASE IN POINT
Carnation Instant promotion

"**I** began as a merchandising specialist at the store level," says Steve Branson, now regional sales coordinator for Carnation Company. "You've seen my type, the guy in the suit who calls on the stores and makes sure they have enough cartons of Carnation Instant Breakfast. I liked the people contact and the company. Eventually, however, I came to the realization that even though I liked my job, I didn't want to spend my whole career stocking shelves and making calls from store to store. I decided it was time to learn and take my career to the next level.

"First, I developed a thorough knowledge of how the organization works. Only when I knew my job cold did I feel comfortable finding ways to expand my influence and argue for new, more efficient ways for us to do business. By looking at what my customers needed, I developed a novel sales strategy which significantly boosted sales in my region. Suddenly, the stores had a value-added service that made a difference.

"Mental role-playing was the key to my promotion," says Steve, who aggressively scheduled meetings with senior management to keep them informed of his progress. "I prepared myself for the next job based on how I distinguished myself before the promotion."

Because your organization might have a certain set of qualities in mind when it promotes employees, the first step should be to see if you fit their criteria, and if you want to. Sketch a realistic picture of your personal skills and abilities. You need to think the same way John did. What do I do well or poorly, and how can I take advantage of my strengths and weaknesses?

▶ *Test yourself: are you ready to move ahead?*

Why did you get hired for your job in the first place?

What do you feel best about in your personal life?

What do you feel worst about in your personal life?

Are your strengths and weaknesses on the job the same as in your personal life?

How will your strengths and weaknesses affect your performance in the next job in your organization?

Do you feel you deserve a promotion?

How do you compare to colleagues of your same generation within the company?

Where do you see yourself in two years, five years?

Is it a promotion you really want?

Don't take a promotion simply for the promotion's sake. As John Stern, one of Sony Corporation's American Officers, says: "I didn't have a promotion in mind when I got my first promotion. Personal growth was my goal. I was looking for something to challenge myself and broaden my experience."

Just because the company thinks you are ready for the job doesn't mean you are. One thing we have learned as managers is that the company may feel that a person is ready for a promotion, but if the person doesn't feel he or she is ready, then most likely, he or she is not ready. We've seen too many cases of "burn-out" among bright, capable, motivated people who didn't realize what the next level of a job entails. So pace yourself. If you get in over your head, let your manager know.

Dennis Hogan, president of Regents/Prentice Hall, spent five years in Los Angeles as an entry-level sales representative before he accepted his first promotion. At times a bit of a jokester, Dennis says that he just wasn't mentally ready for the "grind" of the home office; he was having too much fun surfing! After turning down several opportunities, he eventually accepted one. With his wave-craving behind him, he is now one of the more powerful people at Prentice Hall.

The lesson is: If you are doing your job well enough to be offered a promotion early in your career, chances are your stock in the company will rise if you decide to wait—and keep doing your job. Companies are full of unhappy people who took jobs before they were ready. You must closely examine your strengths, weaknesses, and goals, and consider carefully every opportunity that presents itself.

▶ *Test yourself: Should you take the job?*

1. *The new job*

How much do you know about the job?

Is it an established position, or one that has little definition?

Is it dead-end, or is there upward potential?

Does it broaden your contact with different departments of the company, or is it essentially the same job at a slightly higher level?

What skills are required in the job? Do you enjoy doing those things and are good at them? If not, do you believe that you could learn the skills and be happy with the various responsibilities of the job?

Remember that ambition can sometimes cloud your judgment. Make sure that you are taking the next job for the right reasons—because you enjoy it and see value in it. If you make a move for purely financial reasons, it could be the wrong decision. Think it through.

2. *The people*

With whom would you work, and do you respect them?

What is the manager like? Do you admire and respect that person's capabilities? Could he or she teach and challenge you to grow and improve?

Do you know people who are in or who have had that job? What do they tell you about it? What did they enjoy and what did they describe as the greatest challenge? Are they similar to you?

Are you prepared to act more like a manager with your colleagues than like a friend? Do you have the self-confidence to rely on yourself to get through difficult situations? Do you feel comfortable delegating responsibilities?

Your relationship with people at work changes when you get more responsibility. You may miss being friends with everyone when you have to toe the company line and keep your emotions to yourself. One of the most difficult adjustments can be keeping a poker face so that the other people you work with don't see the stress you are under. Keep it in mind.

3. *The details*

Will the level of travel increase in the next job? If so, are you willing to accept the strain it will place on your personal relationships?

Does the promotion involve a move? If so, is it to an area of the country in which you want to live? Will you be able to maintain your current lifestyle?

How will your financial situation change? Think of your income on a paycheck level. Will you see enough of a gain to offset the hidden costs of a higher-level job (more travel, entertaining, more expensive clothes, etc.)?

With a promotion, there are a lot of little details that you won't learn about until you ask the right questions. Even after you ask all the questions you can think of, there will still be adjustments. That's okay. You'll be able to handle them. Take it one step at a time.

CASE IN POINT
If the suit fits . . .

"I didn't know what I was getting into," said John McNamara, who was promoted to a manager for one of a chain of mid-sized clothing stores. "I had to work long hours—weekends and every holiday. The most difficult part about my promotion is that I had to immediately fire two people. I was also personally responsible for any items that were shoplifted. I liked the extra money, but I wasn't ready for the responsibility or the headaches. If I had asked some questions ahead of time, thought it through, and weighed the trade-offs, I probably wouldn't have taken the job."

After two years, John left retail to do direct-mail marketing for one of Lands' End's competitors. Direct-mail marketing and sales were much more appealing to John. "Looking back, I like the clothing industry," says John. "But I didn't like being on the front line with the customers."

John knows now that he should have taken time to think through what the job really required. (Remember our joke about hindsight?) It's true. Don't think it to death; the right answer is rarely easy to find. And let's be realistic: at times you need a job, any job, and you may not have the luxury of debating all the pros and cons. Sometimes you have to jump in and see if you can swim. All this is natural. It's what your first few years on the job are all about.

The company for life?

Carol has been with Prentice Hall since she graduated from college. She's something of an anomaly. As long as Prentice Hall is able to provide enough challenge and opportunity, she sees no reason to leave.

These days, it's unusual for people to stay at the same company for years. There are other people like Carol who are quite satisfied. Bobbie Jo Buel began her career in journalism at the *Arizona Daily Star* after she graduated from college. Eleven years later, after being promoted from reporter to assistant city editor to features editor to assistant managing editor, she was promoted to managing editor. With over a hundred employees working for her, Bobbie Jo is the second most important manager of the *Star* and she is one of the highest-ranking women in the country in newspaper management.

Tom Kilroy has also been with the same company for twenty years. He began as a sales clerk and is now a vice president and director of sales in the Midwest for Hagger.

"I demonstrated that I had the ability to handle more responsibility and they have continuously given it to me," says Tom, who learned early in his career how to recognize those things which he does well. "Once someone is identified as promotable, each promotion accelerates the next. By staying with the same company, you can develop a track record and lasting relationships."

Whether you stay, go, or look elsewhere depends ultimately on you and your personal goals, your ambitions, and, to some extent, your personality. The changing work environment has certainly made the so-called company man or woman a rarity, but that doesn't mean you shouldn't choose to remain with the same company. What matters most is the extent to which your company does or doesn't stimulate your professional growth. If the company can continue to develop your talents and reward you accordingly, you may decide to stay forever.

Scenario 2. A job with another company in your industry

If you have done well enough to be considered seriously for a promotion, you've probably come to know your current organization fairly well. And since you are considering a move, maybe it's time to confirm your experience by looking at other organizations in your industry.

CASE IN POINT
Writing your own ticket

When we asked Peter Bernstein, editor in chief of *U.S. News & World Report*, how he got his first promotion, he said: "I switched jobs. I started as a reporter for the *New York Daily News* in Queens and went to *Fortune* as associate editor. It was clearly a much better job, with the opportunity to write longer and better stories. Someone starting in this profession needs to have clips and bylines in his or her own name. The job at *Fortune* provided this."

Peter stresses that the most vital part of being promoted or taking a new job is what you bring to it. "Experience isn't as important as intelligence, hard work, and creativity. Just because someone hasn't done a job before doesn't mean he won't be better than someone experienced in that job who brings no imagination to it."

Once you decide to explore a job change, it might be a good idea to heed Peter's advice and consider other companies within your industry. If your company is faring poorly and has a bleak long-term outlook, a promotion may actually hurt your marketability. Why? The simple fact is, if your company is doing poorly, it is much more difficult for any one given individual to be successful. There is also sometimes a stigma attached to being in a level of responsibility at a troubled company. Whether or not you had anything to do with the problems is beside the point. It is similar to being present at the scene of a crime—you're innocent, but you still have to answer questions. Add to this your new higher salary level and you may have trouble finding another job.

After you've proven yourself, your success can bring leveraging power both within your company and out of it. A lot of industries, such as high-technology, are very specialized, and an in-depth knowledge of the market or your job can be hard to replace. If you are fortunate to be in this situation, you have real bargaining power. Perhaps you know some successful people at your company who have made what seem to be extraordinary demands and had them granted, or have left for far better jobs working for a competitor!

CASE IN POINT
Leigh the lever

Leigh Talmage is a vice president with First Interstate Bank. Over two years ago, Leigh received and pursued an attractive offer from another prestigious bank. The other bank offered more money and more responsibility, both of which appealed to Leigh.

"I discussed the offer with my manager in London," said Leigh. "He walked me through the competitive offer and asked me what I needed to stay. I outlined a few of the areas with which I was unhappy and took the opportunity to outline my future goals. Eventually we came to terms.

"Without the competitive offer, he might not have known how serious I was about improving my current job status and brightening my future. My advice in these matters is simple: If you are ready to walk and you're worth keeping, your employer will have to listen and take action."

The whole enchilada

The moral here is obvious: Don't sell yourself short. You can't afford to work for a company that can't give you the opportunities you merit. Jennifer Scruby recently landed a new job as an assistant beauty editor at *Vogue* magazine. The job came after a successful first job at an ad agency and an editorial job at *Lear's* magazine.

"Even though I was doing well and making more money at the ad agency, I wasn't happy with the work environment and stress level. I decided to take a step back and give magazine writing a try, since I am interested in fashion and majored in English. The job at *Lear's* was a good start, but given my background and experience, I thought I was qualified for the best. However, when I heard about the job opening at *Vogue*, it wasn't entirely an easy decision. I had only been at *Lear's* for a few months and had been at the ad agency for a little over a year. I was worried how it might look. Eventually, however, I realized the risk was worth it for the level of prestige and challenge of *Vogue*."

▶ *Reality check: to leave or not to leave?*

What is the company's current position in the industry? Does its revenue come from one product or division or many divisions? Which division would you work in?

What major product or plans does your company have in development? Would you characterize your company as innovative or conservative?

What do you think of management? Do you like and respect the employees? Do you look up to senior management? Do they respect and believe in you?

Has management been reorganized at any time in the last six months? Are reorganizations frequent? Is the position you are considering the result of a reorganization?

The bottom line is: it's important for you to analyze if your current company is worthy of your best efforts. Talented people today have lots of opportunities. Your sense of pride and integrity demand that you work for a company that will give as much to you—through recognition, opportunity for growth, and compensation—as you are willing to give to it.

Scenario 3. A job in another industry

So what happens when you've been at your first job for a few years and you get itchy to try something else? Carol's brother Craig (in case you're keeping track, she has four brothers) was a reporter for *Fortune* magazine before he decided to go to business school and specialize in marketing. He now works for Motorola, where he markets the smallest portable phone in the world.

Does this sound like a far cry from journalism? It is. But after reporting on business for a few years, Craig decided he wanted to be part of it.

While your skills and experience may be immediately transferable to another company within your industry, they may be even more valuable to a company in a related or unrelated industry. Such was the case two years ago when Gary left textbooks for software. He had come to know the ins and outs of college textbooks—in particular, textbooks on software and computers—but he wasn't aware how much his experience was worth until he began talking to software companies. They had no trouble finding people who knew software, marketing, or the textbook industry, but the combination of all three was difficult to find. He jumped ship for a better working environment and more money, and his skills had an immediate impact on his new company's success.

"Know when to leave a job if you're unhappy," says Jordan Simon, project manager for Venture West Real Estate Company. "But leave for the right reasons. It's easy to become desperate if you don't have a job. So, unless the conditions are unbearable, stay with your present job and do a search in due time. People seldom make good decisions when they are angry or upset."

Jordan has a good point. A new job or industry won't solve a fundamental unhappiness in your personal life. As you consider your next move, take a moment to make sure you are changing for the right reason. Do you like your job, from both a micro and a macro level; i.e., do you like what you're doing and why you're doing it? If the answer is no to either question, you may be fooling yourself into thinking a move outside your industry will make you happier. Look around! It can't hurt. It will only make your decision to stay or go more certain.

TIPS FOR CONSIDERING OTHER INDUSTRIES

1. *Figure out what you have to sell.* What do you do well that you can offer other industries? If you sell pencils, would you enjoy selling coloring books? If you have good people skills, would you enjoy sales? We've seen some unusual matches: teachers who have become great sales people; insurance-claims adjusters who have made great teachers; etc. The most important questions to ask are: What am I fundamentally good at, and where can I build a case for my skills?

2. *If you're going to travel, travel first class.* Don't go to a shrinking industry or a poorly managed company, even for more money. Just as a rising tide raises all ships, a sinking one lowers them. Make sure you trade up. Tim Vertovec, an editor at our company, left a year ago to take a job with one of our competitors on the West Coast. The job paid more, the location (San Diego) was key, but the company's finances were in dire straits. About six months after he left, his new company closed their San Diego office and he was forced to move to Fort Worth, Texas. He certainly had not anticipated making another move. Some decisions are out of your control, including the actions an organization in trouble will take to cure its ills.

3. *Be realistic.* Pick a job you know you can do. Don't think a job change is going to make you magically better or worse at a particular area.

4. *Shop around.* Look at all related industries. If you decide to go into advertising, take a look at public relations. In many cases, jobs are similar across industries, and your knowledge of related areas will help.

Scenario 4. Back to school or beyond

The nineties, "the hangover decade," as Tom Wolfe refers to it, will see a return to basic principles and a rejection of the high-flying hedonistic eighties. More and more, people are putting their careers on hold and pursuing life-long dreams while they are young. We are strong supporters of adventure, of being happy and fulfilled. That's why we wrote this book. The ultimate message we hope you take away is that success is measured by personal fulfillment, not in dollars, material goods, or titles.

It could be that the change your life needs is radical. That's fine, but we urge you to apply the same caution and thought processes in approaching the radical change of going back to school or taking time off to travel as you apply to considering the incremental change of a new job or promotion.

CASE IN POINT
Suni on the lam

One of Gary's close friends, Suni Yang, recently took a year-long leave of absence from her job as an electrical engineer at Hewlett-Packard to travel around the world. Suni was a top performer in Hewlett-Packard's microwave division. She had an undergraduate and a graduate degree in electrical engineering from Stanford and was on the promotion track at Hewlett-Packard.

"I wasn't sure I wanted to be an engineer for the rest of my life. And one of my life-long goals was to travel around the world, starting in New Zealand, where I spent three months after school. I am not sure what I will do when I get back, that's why I am on the trip."

One of the biggest questions we all face is whether what we are doing matters. Having all the options in the world open to you can be stifling, and there is no easy way to know ahead of time if your choices will make you happy. Suni's trip helped her to clarify her immediate and her long-term goals. Sometimes a change of scenery—if only for a week or a weekend—can change your attitude and your outlook. Listen to yourself when you need those changes, and plan accordingly.

Back to school

Should you go back to school? Almost all the people we know have asked themselves that question at one time or another, and many have gone back to try it out. But before you jump back into the academic cradle, take a moment to ponder why. There are only two valid reasons for going back:

1. To get advanced training to help you in your current job: an undergraduate degree, an MBA, or a specialized degree
2. To change careers: to go into law, medicine, etc.

After a couple of years as an accountant, and a few years as a writer for *Connoisseur* magazine, Mary Vandeveire decided to return to school to get her Master's in broadcast journalism. "I love to write and I like the excitement of live reporting," says Mary, who just completed her first year of graduate school at Columbia. While in school, Mary has worked part-time at a local news network, and she's run a number of publicity and promotional campaigns.

Carol's brother Kent worked as a congressional aide on Capitol Hill for a few years before he went to law school. He learned a lot about what our senators and congressmen do and he saw firsthand how groups in Washington do business, such as special-interests groups, political-action committees, and others. In addition to his experience on the Hill, he also worked for the National Urban League. By the time he was ready to start law school, he had a new perspective to bring to the classroom. That served him well in school and at interviewing time when he got his first job.

Jane Dobson also decided to return to school to get her law degree after working for a few years. "I've never felt there's just one career I'd been interested in," says Jane, who was in advertising before she started law school. "I have a lot of interests and for now I've whittled them down to the general area of law. Although I'm an environmental lawyer, there are a number of paths I can take from here. I don't see myself doing the same job for the next forty years."

Try it, you'll like it

Unlike other alternatives, you can try school before making a full-time commitment. Take a few part-time classes in the area you're interested in, before you commit yourself to going full-time. If you are lucky, the organization you work for will even pay for the courses. Too many people quit their jobs and go back to school without knowing what it will be like.

▸ *Test yourself*

What are you giving up personally and financially? You will have less money—not just the money it costs to go to school, but also the money you would have earned.

Is the degree you are pursuing a necessity for your future success? Obviously, you can't be a doctor without a medical degree, but there are a lot of people with MBAs who don't use them.

Are you going back to school to escape, or are you really interested in the area you'll study? School does not offer relief from the daily pressures of work or of building a life. What is your real reason for going back?

TIPS FOR GOING BACK TO SCHOOL

1. *Don't go back to school as a solution in itself.* Your degree should be part of a long-term plan, not an end in itself. Your goal doesn't matter—whether it is to run your company, save the rain forests, or heal the sick. Not having a goal does, because you'll leave school poorer financially and no better off than when you went in.

2. *Go back with experience.* Don't make the mistake of undervaluing the experience you've had before or after school. The types of problems and skills involved in your job do help frame your school experience. When Gary went back to take a computer class, he was surprised that he had learned a lot of computer skills at work. The class fine-tuned his already solid knowledge base.

3. *Network.* School is a great place to meet future co-workers, business partners, or even bosses. Now that you have had a chance to see how important networking can be, don't forget it when you get back in the classroom.

Alternate means of support: Finding your niche in the world

Going to school or working for a biweekly paycheck aren't your only options. There are other very viable means of earning a good living, either by starting your own business or by freelancing your skills. We don't have space, within the scope of this book, to write a complete guide to starting your own business; there are a million guides along those lines. We do, however, want to dismiss the myth that you can't start your own business until you have years of experience.

Flattening, efficient organizations mean more contract jobs

As organizations of all kinds—hospitals, schools, law offices, banks, to name a few—continue to emphasize cost-cutting and efficiency, they will increase their freelance, work-for-hire contracts. These types of contracts save money because businesses do not have to pay freelance workers benefits. They are also easier to account for; i.e., you can assign costs to a particular project. Finally, as the working population ages, more and more part-time workers will pour into the market. If you are a skilled worker—a designer, a computer programmer, or a writer— you may be in good shape to break out on your own.

Technology is slowly eliminating the central office

As computers appear in every home and their power and access via telecommunication lines increase, more and more work will be done at home or off-site. Companies can save large amounts of money on leasing space and on insurance, and, in many cases, achieve higher levels of productivity. As we have mentioned, technology managed well can make people enormously efficient. When mismanaged, however, it can hinder what people are able to accomplish.

Complex tasks are being completed in less time

Four or five years ago, a company may have needed a full-time designer or programmer, but now computer tools have increased productivity and eliminated full-time jobs. The demand for these jobs is still there; they just don't take as long to complete.

▸ *Test yourself: out on your own?*

Are you a self-starter? If you need the support of an office and the structure of job responsibilities and a boss, don't even think of starting your own business.

Are you accomplished? Organizations are willing to let employees learn on the job. With freelancers, they expect a job done to perfection. They will also want proof of your work before they hire you.

Will you have to drum up business? Are you good at selling yourself and your ideas? Starting from scratch is difficult.

Do you have the support and wherewithal to make it?

Starting and successfully running your own business, whether it is freelancing or a full-time occupation, takes a tremendous amount of maturity. You have to deal with complex financial issues, bulletproof deadlines, and angry customers. For most people, this maturity comes after many years on a full-time job. Only a few people have the courage and aptitude to take it on at an early age. For every Bill Gates, who started Microsoft at nineteen, there are a million failures. We are not trying to scare you away—certainly, there will be more opportunities for entrepreneurs in the future. Just remember how hard it is.

Is this the right time?

Before you leap a hundred feet when the company says jump, move to another industry, or head back to campus, think about whether or not this move is right for you personally as well as professionally. Promotions mean more responsibility, more work, and usually greater skill. The older you get, the more weight people attach to your decisions and the outcome of a particular job. They assume you will make those decisions more maturely. Don't let their expectations sink, but do what's right for you. It can be a tough call, but if you continue to question yourself and your motives and doggedly seek the advice of others, you'll make the best choices. Most of all, do what makes you feel good about yourself, and whether it's a new job, school, or a completely different track, consider the implications of your decision before you make it.

And as much as we wish it weren't true, as mortals we're inhibited by circumstances. For example, one of Carol's friends works for a major financial company. Eventually, he'd like to start his own business and be free of the shackles of big business. But for now he's intent on staying with his company so that he can test out his ideas for a small business of his own. He wants to have a fully developed business plan, and he wants to save a chunk of money on the job he has now.

Taking the long path

Don't you wish sometimes someone would tell you what to do with the rest of your life, so you could go do it without worrying? We all do. Unfortunately, that will not happen. But there also is no wrong path to take, provided you consider your options carefully. Edie Faubert taught special education for five years and then went into the retail business. She learned a lot from retail, but over a period of time she felt it didn't fulfill her need to help people. She returned to special education after five years. "I want to make a contribution," says Edie, who is thirty-three. "The older I get, the more I realize how important it is for me to do something that I enjoy which also enables me to help others. Working with special-education children and their parents is the best way for me to use my abilities and my advantages."

John Dineen graduated from high school and spent five years as a tugboat captain before attending community college and then transferring to Harvard. After a stint in commercial real estate and a year of business school, he dropped out to work full-time in the financial industry. He had little idea he'd move from guiding ships in Los Angeles Harbor to analyzing balance sheets on Wall Street. But at each step, he took his time, made up his mind as best he could, and moved ahead. Everything has turned out fine.

Be open to opportunities

Do you have to recognize all the opportunities in life ahead of time? Of course not. For all your planning and foresight, there will be certain opportunities which fall in your lap. Maintaining an open outlook and relying on your intuition will make it possible for you to weigh these prospects and determine if the timing is right for you to act.

CASE IN POINT
Scott Carter, stand-up comedian

Carol's brother Scott was a stand-up comedian in New York for five years. His progress was slow but steady. Eventually, he felt frustrated writing for himself as a stand-up, and he began to apply for jobs as a comedy writer. One of his friends got him a break writing for an HBO show. After a few weeks, the higher-ups noticed his talent and offered him a permanent job as a writer. Now, three short years later, Scott is an executive producer for HBO. He is in charge of three of their comedy shows. Although he never imagined himself in TV production, he's found the best use for his varied talents: writing, managing people, and being creative. Most important, he loves the work.

Lots of people take circuitous paths to their perfect careers. Some people have had numerous careers, all of which they enjoy. In fact, the average person changes his or her career five times during the course of a lifetime. Others stay with the same job and bring imagination and creativity to it for as long as fifty years. Over the next few years, you'll determine which path—or paths—is for you.

Making a difference

Nothing is more difficult, more exhilarating, more rewarding, and sometimes more fleeting than achieving a sense of accomplishment, whether it's in your job or in your personal life. John Gardner, speaking at the hundredth commencement at Stanford, offered advice to three thousand graduates weighing their career and life choices:

"Life isn't a mountain that has a summit. Nor a game that has a final score. Life is an endless unfolding, and, if we wish it to be, an endless process of self-discovery, an endless and unpredictable dialogue between one's own potentiality and the life situations in which we find ourselves. The United States is facing a test of character. The test is whether in all the confusion and clash of interests, all the distracting conflicts and cross-purposes, all the temptations and self-indulgence and self-exoneration, we have the strength of purpose, the guts, the convictions, the spiritual staying power to build a future worthy of our past."

EIGHT

The Big Picture:

Understanding the World

of the Nineties

Even if you're on the right track, you'll get run over if you just sit there.

—Will Rogers

That is happiness; to be absorbed into something complete and great.

—Willa Cather

If we are to achieve a rich culture, rich in contrasting values, we must recognize the whole gamut of human potentialities, and so weave a less arbitrary social fabric, one in which each diverse human gift will find a fitting place.   *—Margaret Mead*

As you're settling into your life and your job after college, you'll also be adjusting to the world outside the classroom. At the same time as you are adjusting, a number of issues and trends are emerging that will change our world and the way we work. We thought it would be helpful to discuss some of these patterns as a means of concluding this book. These trends are interesting because they present both challenge and opportunity. How we respond to them will have a great impact on the world of tomorrow.

The global vision

"The new electronic interdependence re-creates the world in the image of a global village."   —Marshall McLuhan

The world is interconnected economically and politically more than ever before. The United States fights to protect interests in the Middle East. Coca-Cola sales increase abroad more than in this country. General Motors manufactures cars in Europe and in Mexico. The world's leaders meet in Rio de Janeiro for an international summit on the environment. Increasingly, our very livelihood depends on our international neighbors.

CASE IN POINT
Man of the year

In 1991, *Time* magazine named Ted Turner Man of the Year. Why? Because he was able to exploit new technology, including satellites, to make the media truly global. You could have been in Japan during the Persian Gulf War and viewed full coverage on CNN. You could have been in Mexico City, as Carol was, as the Soviet Union fell apart, and seen the whole story as though you were there.

Ted Turner is a pioneer of global business. He understood early on that, however people differ, they share common interests around the world. People in Eastern Europe want to know what is happening in the United States. Brazilians want to know what the Japanese are doing—in their spare time as well as on the job.

Think of all the economic changes that have taken place in the last few years. Europe is bound together as one economic force. The United States is working more closely than ever with Mexico and Canada. Although there are still some countries like China which are ruled by Communist systems, more and more countries are opening up to free trade. That means more opportunities for people in more countries than ever before, and increased competition here in America as those same countries try to win a share of the large United States market. We'll have to be better than we have ever been—smarter at developing the best ideas, and better at delivering quality in time, to compete and win. We'll have to understand more about people who are different from us—people from developing countries, people who don't speak English. People we can learn from, no matter what their language. That's an exciting, dynamic challenge.

Quality and competition

"Quality never goes out of style."   —*Levi Strauss*

One country that fully understands the global market is Japan. In the years after World War II, the Japanese have set a new standard of quality and achievement. They took a country in ruins and built it into one of the most powerful economic forces in the world, in less than fifty years. From Nissan to Sony, they have consistently developed and manufactured products which are recognized throughout the world as being of the highest quality.

CASE IN POINT
The junkyard engineer

Soichiro Honda is best known as the founder and driving force of Honda Motor Company, Ltd. At the end of World War II, he was an out-of-work engineer with a lot of ambition and patriotic energy, but no money. Honda built his first motorcycle out of scrap parts he found in a junkyard. After perfecting a design, he put the motorcycle into production and sold millions to space-conscious Japanese, and eventually to the world.

After a few years, he built his first automobile assembly plant. Up against dominant American manufacturers, Honda knew he had to distinguish his product by something other than price or style. He turned to quality. He perfected a new style of car manufacturing that put quality before quantity and placed the burden on the individual worker and his production team. Last year, cars from Honda were the best-selling imports in the United States, and the Honda Accord was the best-selling car in America.

For America to compete with Japan and the European Economic Community, we will have to return to the fundamentals. As simple as that may sound, we will have to develop and build products that people want to buy. In the nineties, that means quality products that last. We have the potential to be as good or better than the Japanese in our commitment to quality, provided we get off our high horse and take no markets for granted: quality work, quality products, quality services, and quality outcomes.

You have the ability to contribute to this standard of excellence by doing the best job you can. If you take pride in your work, if you pay attention to every detail and treat every person with care along the way, then you will create a quality product. Your behavior will set the example.

Economic inequality and the quality of life

"I think Capitalism, wisely managed, can probably be made more efficient for attaining economic ends than any alternative system yet in sight, but that in itself is, in many ways, extremely objectionable." —*John Maynard Keynes*

Even though external pressures and competition are increasing, the American system, fundamentally based on capitalism, is still a wonder of modern society. Few countries enjoy our wealth, power, and security. In recent decades, however, the myth of the American Dream has begun to play itself out. The dollar buys much less than it used to, and we are all having to work harder than our parents did, just to maintain a lifestyle similar to theirs.

Unlike the do-anything-to-make-a-lot of-money eighties, the nineties will respond to the internal pressure of changing economic distribution with much more thought and deliberation. From the streets of Los Angeles to the corporate boardrooms, fairness and quality of life are becoming much bigger issues. CEOs are being asked to take pay cuts and earn their bonuses by improving company performance. All public figures are under close financial scrutiny. People are realizing they have less and are speaking up.

For our part, the prospect of having less than our parents is redirecting our priorities. More and more people are concerned with what kind of contribution they will make in their life. People are spending time evaluating what is important to them—in their life and on the job—whether it's staying home to raise their children or exchanging leisure activities for work.

Cultural diversity and the community

"We must learn to live together as brothers or perish as fools."
—Martin Luther King, Jr.

America's ethnic fabric will become increasingly more diverse. According to the Bureau of Labor Statistics, twenty years from now the white population will peak at 195 million and will begin to decline in numbers. Two significant groups—Asian Americans and African Americans—will rival the largest minority, the Hispanic population. More of the United States will become what San Francisco, Chicago, and New York have been for years—culturally diverse melting pots. Whatever your cultural and ethnic background is, you will have to understand both differences and similarities among people. The more open-minded you are, the more you will learn of what different people have to teach you.

American businesses have a mandate to hire people who reflect this diversity. Gone are the days of the all-white male staffs so prevalent in the fifties and sixties, when your parents and grandparents were working. Be aware that companies will be looking for people who value and promote diversity. Diversity in the workplace will also mean more opportunities for handicapped and disabled people.

Education

"Education is what survives when what has been learned has been forgotten."

—*B. F. Skinner*

Johnette Moore was Carol's art teacher in grade school. She was the first person to teach her to draw and to explain the techniques of the master artists. Carol saw Johnette a few months ago near her home in Lewiston, Idaho. Johnette now teaches sixth-graders everything from geography and literature to science.

While Carol, Johnette, and her husband and son had dinner, Carol was thinking that there is nothing more important than the effect a good teacher can have on a student. Johnette, like a few other teachers Carol had, not only taught her the subject matter at hand; she also taught her how to do her best, how to keep trying, and at times how to behave. (Carol and her friends sometimes liked to talk during class.)

Teachers are the heroes of our country. Teachers have the ability to shape young minds more positively than any other single group. In the next few years, our society, we hope, will provide greater support for education and reward the best teachers for the contributions they make.

Education in America will be a critical concern in the nineties. Why? With high school dropout rates approaching fifty percent in some urban areas, in a nation plagued with illiteracy (some people say one out of every four can't read), Americans just aren't getting the education they need to compete. State and local school districts have cut budgets in the recession of the late eighties and the early nineties, but corporations rapidly increased the amount of money they spend on employee training. Community-college enrollment increased eight percent during the early nineties—much of it from corporate-sponsored courses. Indeed, some companies are paying colleges to teach undergraduate and graduate courses in the workplace.

Recent international tests show that American students are well behind most European and Japanese students in math and science aptitude. Is it any wonder that we are losing the economic battle? Our single most important resource is our youth. How well we develop their minds, their talents, and their abilities will determine whether America continues to be a world power.

The environment

"No such thing as Internal Affairs remains on earth. Mankind's salvation lies exclusively in everyone making everything his business."   —*Aleksandr Solzhenitsyn*

In Carol's household, they buy recycled toilet paper, napkins, and paper towels. We recycle our newspapers and our bottles and cans. At work, we've begun to use the other sides of paper for scratch pads. We recycle file folders instead of throwing them in the garbage after one use. Our habits are changing in small ways. But small steps eventually yield big differences.

We are in the midst of a global environmental crisis, from the rain forests of South America to the hole in the ozone above Antarctica. In the nineties, the crisis will become much more local. Excesses like the Exxon Valdez oil spill and the destruction of the Kuwaiti oil fields will pale in comparison to increased skin and other cancers, air and water pollution, accelerated population growth, and the continued destruction of wild lands.

On a national level, business and government will be forced to confront these issues through legislation and regulation. Locally, recycling and management of household wastes will become mandatory. Some companies, like Chevron, have trained over three thousand managers in all areas of the company to think about the environmental ramifications of everything they do. We predict that other companies will follow suit. Maintaining the environment and taking steps to solve existing problems are everyone's responsibility.

Technology

"As with any set of tools, the real power of information technology comes from the human ideas that create and focus it."
   —*Arno Penzias, Nobel Prize-winning physicist, author of* Ideas and Information

Star Wars, lunar colonies, and computers with personalities are all still in the future, but technology will continue to change the way we work and live. At work, everyone will embrace the computer and telecommunication technologies. It is likely that some major portion of your job will be supported, replaced, or made more efficient by advances in technology. Because technology allows us to do more and do it better and quicker (think, for example, about the effect of computers on the publishing industry), there will be more pressure for us to create quality work on time. In fact, your whole career could depend on how well you understand and use the technology and anticipate the changes that are coming.

At home, the change will be slower, but with more serious implications. Biotechnology is likely to extend our life spans (more people live to be over a hundred years old than ever before, almost a forty percent increase in the last forty years). Longevity will require us to plan better for our old age. We will need to reevaluate social programs like Medicare and Social Security. More important, we will need to pace our lives better and plan our careers more carefully.

Without the computer, it would have taken us two to three more years to finish this book. Working with one disk, we passed it back and forth as we made changes and corrections. Because we had a laser printer, it was much easier to print the manuscript and read the hard copy as we worked. The process of writing was still long and tedious, but it was made easier because of technology. Who knows how much easier it may become to write in the next ten years?

The job isn't just a job anymore

What do all these things mean for you and your daily routine? Companies have realized that people buy things for reasons that don't always have to do with the product's quality. They may want to help the environment or the homeless, or they may want to own the latest technology, just for technology's sake. Companies have also realized that the problems the world faces are beyond the scope of government. And they are stepping in to fill part of the gap themselves.

Even in our business, we realize that we have to work hard to identify initiatives in education that make a difference, in addition to producing great books and teaching programs. If people don't understand Prentice Hall's mission and why we are leaders in the field of education, then why should they believe us and work with us?

CASE IN POINT
Socially conscious ice cream

Do you ever have Ben & Jerry's ice cream? Did you know that there is a lot more to Ben & Jerry's than high-quality ice cream? Ben and Jerry both believe in distributing their profits more equitably than companies traditionally do. At their company, the highest-paid executive cannot earn more than five times the salary of the lowest-paid worker. Recently, they had an opening for a vice president of marketing, and they were prepared to let it go unfilled for two years if they couldn't find anyone to take the job at $75,000 a year.

They've given of their proceeds to the homeless and recently have committed themselves to donating forty percent of the proceeds from their Rain Forest Crunch ice cream to saving the rain forests in Brazil. All the while, they have continued to be a favorite company on Wall Street. Their stock, along with their earnings, continues to rise.

The Russell Athletic Company, makers of sportswear, feels strongly about helping high school students stay in school and graduate. Their "Stay in School" campaign reflects their priorities as a company and has been the focal point of all their advertising campaigns.

And they're not the only ones. There are plenty of companies and people at those companies who are trying to combine business and a good cause. Not all jobs lend themselves as easily to altruism, but if you assume responsibility for thinking how you can make a difference in the world, then you will.

CASE IN POINT
Running for relief

Linda Montag, a vice president of a German bank, decided to make a difference on her vacation. An avid runner, Linda joined the World Runners club, a group which uses running as a means to help end world hunger.

"People look for additional satisfaction in their lives," says Linda, who learned firsthand about Thailand through her experience as a fund raiser and as a volunteer. On her three-week vacation, Linda joined nine other Americans who were also World Runners. "We joined forces with the Nutritional Institute, which identified the villages that needed our help most. We raised money before our trip which was used for soybean milk, sanitation improvements, and for building a school. In addition to our half-marathon run, we worked each day in the village to help complete an addition to an existing school.

"Travel, as well as running, is one of my passions," says Linda. "This was one of the best ways to truly see and understand the people of Thailand, instead of just flying in and out of Bangkok after seeing a few temples." You can combine several goals—helping others, seeing the world, participating in a sport. You just have to think about the goals at the outset and plan accordingly.

There are all kinds of other people making a difference in their spare time. Bebe Johnson, a self-employed interior designer, took one week off with her father last year and worked for Habitat for Humanity. They built low-income housing for people in Tennessee. Jerry Callaghan is president of Shearson Lehman Hutton. Each year, he sponsors high school students who are going to college. If they get in, he pays their tuition. Vincent Perez sponsors orphaned children in the Philippines. Terry Voltz raises money for kids with multiple sclerosis by riding his bike in bikathons. Susan Flynn teaches English as a second language to Latins who have just come to this country. David Gillespie spends a day a month with a disadvantaged boy through the Big Brothers program. Rob McCarry and his wife, Cle, make sandwiches for the homeless each Thanksgiving and pass them out on the streets of New York.

It all comes back to you

With so much going on in your personal life, at work, and in the world, it is easy to get confused and wonder what life is all about. That's a question you may ask in your first year out of college or your fiftieth. Change is the only constant and it's healthy to question your personal priorities in light of what's happening in the world. But when all the issues get sorted out and push comes to shove, the only one who can change your life is you.

Carol recently spoke with a friend of hers who was applying for a new job in her company. The company told her that, although she was qualified for the particular job, they were going to conduct an outside search. This woman's husband has his own business. They have one child and would like to have more. So she is weighing not only her career goals but also her personal aspirations. "I understand," she said. "But I know that I am the best person for that job and that I really want it—with my whole heart. And if I don't get it, it's not meant to be. But I don't like what I'm doing now. It's not the right fit."

"It sounds like you have it all in perspective," Carol said, trying to be encouraging.

"I feel really good about myself," said the woman. "I know I'm being true to myself. I refuse to stay in a situation which doesn't make me happy. I'm better than that."

Indeed, she was better than her current job. What Carol's friend has is self-respect and the presence of mind to know what she wants and pursue it. As you think about your job and your life in the next few years, strive to do your best. But remember your heart—your sense of self, your goals, your dreams, and your special talents. Seek a job and a career that will be satisfying, something which you will enjoy every day.

But please don't stop with yourself. Think about your responsibility to the community, to the causes you believe in, and to the future of the world. You can and should make a difference in your own way. Live the complete life that will allow you to look back someday and say: I'm proud of what I've done.

Professional Associations

and Recreational and Special-Interest

Organizations

Below are a number of organizations which you may be interested in joining. You can write or call to find out what they do and what specific programs and functions you may be able to attend. There are other obvious organizations—such as your local alumni or alumnae club—which you may also want to join. Organizations such as these provide a great opportunity for making friends, learning new things, and making career contacts.

Professional Associations

Accounting

Accreditation Council for Accounting
    1010 N. Fairfax St.
    Alexandria, VA 22314
    (703) 549-6400
    Robert N. Bradshaw, Accreditation Dir.

American Accounting Association
    5717 Bessie Dr.
    Sarasota, FL 34233
    (813) 921-7747
    Paul L. Gerhardt, Exec. Dir.

American Association of Hispanic CPAs
    1414 Metropolitan Ave.
    Bronx, NY 10462
    (212) 823-6144
    Robert Rosario, Contact

American Society of Women Accountants
  35 E. Wacker Dr., Suite 1068
  Chicago, IL 60601
  (312) 726-9030
  Miriam Greene, Exec. Dir.

Asian American Certified Public Accountants
  543-9 Green Ridge Dr.
  Daly City, CA 94014
  (415) 957-3000
  Tiffany Hong, Pres.

Advertising

Advertising Club of New York
  155 E. 55th St., Suite 202
  New York, NY 10022
  (212) 935-8080
  Denise Harbin, Exec. Dir.

Advertising Photographers of America
  27 W. 20th St.
  New York, NY 10011

Advertising Women of New York
  153 E. 57th St.
  New York, NY 10022
  (212) 593-1950
  Lee Carpenter, Exec. Dir.

Association of Independent Commercial Producers
  Kaufman Astoria Studios
  34-12 36th St.
  Astoria, NY 11106
  (718) 392-2427
  Melissa Angerman, Exec. Dir.

Young Professionals Division (Advertising)
  c/o Advertising Club of New York
  155 E. 55th St., Suite 202
  New York, NY 10022
  (212) 935-8080
  Steve Kaufman, Pres.

Architecture

American Institute of Architects
1735 New York Ave., NW
Washington, DC 20006
(202) 626-7300
James P. Cramer, CEO

American Institute of Architecture Students
1735 New York Ave., NW
Washington, DC 20006
(202) 626-7472
Carl D. Costello, Exec. Dir.

Education Futures, Inc. (Architecture)
2118 Spruce St.
Philadelphia, PA 19103

Aviation

Aircraft Owners and Pilot Association
421 Aviation Way
Frederick, MD 21701
(301) 695-2000
John L. Baker, Pres.

Council of Defense and Space Industry Associations
1722 I St., NW, Suite 300
Washington, DC 20006
(202) 457-8713
Jean A. Caffiaux, Exec. Sec.

Future Aviation Professionals of America
4959 Massachusetts Blvd.
Atlanta, GA 30337
(404) 997-8097
William Louis Smith, Pres.

Banking

National Association of Bank Women
  500 N. Michigan Ave., Suite 1400
  Chicago, IL 60611
  (312) 661-1700
  Doris Payne, Exec. Dir.

National Association of Urban Bankers
  122 C St., NW, Suite 580
  Washington, DC 20001
  (202) 783-4743
  Lethia A. Kelly, Exec. Dir.

Business

American Society of Professional & Executive Women
  1429 Walnut St.
  Philadelphia, PA 19102
  (215) 563-4415
  Laurie Wagman, Exec. Dir.

Association of Collegiate Entrepreneurs
  1845 N. Fairmount
  Box 147
  Wichita, KS 67208
  (316) 689-3000
  Donald Herman, Dir.

Executive Women International
  Spring Run Executive Plaza
  965 East 4800, Suite 1
  Salt Lake City, UT 84117
  (801) 263-3296
  Patricia Parilla, Pres.

Inventors Association of America
  P.O. Box 1531
  Rancho Cucamonga, CA 91730
  (714) 980-6446
  L. Troy Hall, Pres.

National Association of Asian American Professionals
P.O. Box 772
New York, NY 10002
(212) 533-9335
John Chang, Pres.

National Association of Business Economists
28790 Chagrin Blvd., Suite 300
Cleveland, OH 44122
(216) 464-7986
David L. Williams, Exec. Dir.

National Black MBA Association
180 N. Michigan Ave., Suite 1820
Chicago, IL 60601
(312) 236-2622
Leroy D. Nunery, Pres.

National Minority Business Council
235 E. 42nd St.
New York, NY 10017
(212) 573-2385
John F. Robinson, CEO & Pres.

Powerlunch!
3701 Connecticut Ave., NW, Suite 622
Washington, DC 20008
(202) 966-8334
Sandy A. Crowe, Pres.

Professional Salespersons of America
3801 Monaco, NE
Albuquerque, NM 87111

Engineering

American Indian Science and Engineering Society
1085 14th St., Suite 1506
Boulder, CO 80302
(303) 492-8658
Norbert S. Hill, Jr., Exec. Dir.

American Institute of Chemical Engineers
345 E. 47th St.
New York, NY 10017

American Society of Civil Engineers
345 E. 47th St.
New York, NY 10017
(212) 705-7496
Dr. Edward O. Pfrany, Exec. Dir.

American Society of Mechanical Engineers
345 E. 47th St.
New York, NY 10017
(212) 705-7722
Dr. David Belden, Exec. Dir.

Biomedical Engineering Society
P.O. Box 2399
Culver City, CA 9231

Institute of Electrical and Electronic Engineers
345 E. 47th St.
New York, NY 10017
(212) 705-7900
Eric Herz, Gen. Mgr.

National Society of Black Engineers
344 Commerce St.
Alexandria, VA 22314
(703) 549-2207
Florida Morehead, Exec. Dir.

Society of Hispanic Professional Engineers
5400 E. Olympic Blvd., Suite 225
Los Angeles, CA 90022
(213) 725-3970

Society of Women Engineers
345 E. 47th St., Room 305
New York, NY 10017
(212) 705-7855
B.J. Harrod, Acting Exec. Dir.

Fashion

American Fashion Association
  Dallas Fashion Mart, Suite 5442
  Dallas, TX 75258
  (214) 631-0821
  Bette Hamilton, Exec. Admin.

Council of Fashion Designers of America
  1412 Broadway, Suite 1006
  New York, NY 10018
  (212) 302-1821
  Robert Raymond, Exec. Dir.

Finance

American Finance Association
  Graduate School of Business Admin.
  100 Trinity Pl.
  New York Univ.
  New York, NY 10006
  (212) 285-8915
  Michael Keenan, Exec. Sec./Treas.

Financial Women's Association of New York
  215 Park Ave. S., Suite 2014
  New York, NY 10003
  (212) 533-2141
  Nancy Sellar, Exec. Dir.

Stockholders of America
  1625 Eye St., NW, Suite 724A
  Washington, DC 20006
  (202) 783-3430
  Margaret Cox Sullivan, Pres.

Graphic Arts

American Institute of Graphic Arts
  1059 Third Ave.
  New York, NY 10021
  (212) 752-0813
  Caroline Hightower, Exec. Dir.

Young Printing Executives Club of New York (Graphic Arts)
Five Penn Plaza
New York, NY 10001
(212) 279-2100
William A. Dirzulaitis, Exec. Officer

Law

American Bar Association Young Lawyers Division
750 N. Lake Shore Dr.
Chicago, IL 60611
(312) 947-4103
Ron Hirsch, Staff Dir.

American Society of International Law
2223 Massachusetts Ave., NW
Washington, DC 20008
(202) 265-4313
John Lawrence Hargrove, Exec. Dir.

International Law Students Association
2223 Massachusetts Ave., NW
Washington, DC 20008-2864
(202) 797-7133
Denise M. Hodge, Exec. Dir.

Management/Marketing

Association of Human Resource Systems Professionals
P.O. Box 801646
Dallas, TX 75380
(214) 661-3727
James D. Stroop, Exec. Dir.

American Marketing Association
250 S. Wacker Dr., Suite 200
Chicago, IL 60606

Center for Creative Leadership
P.O. Box P-1
5000 Laurinda Dr.
Greensboro, NC 27402-1660

Center for Management Effectiveness
427 Beirut Ave.
Pacific Palisades, CA 90272

National Association of Career Development Consultants
1707 L St., NW, Suite 333
Washington, DC 20036
(202) 452-9102
Betsy Houston, Exec. Dir.

Media

Academy of Television Arts and Sciences
3500 W. Olive Ave., Suite 700
Burbank, CA 91505
(818) 953-7575
James L. Loper, Exec. Dir.

American College of Radio Marketing
710 Avendell, Suite 103
P.O. Box 1801
Morehead City, NC 28557
(919) 247-7131
Charles Campbell, Pres.

American Society of Magazine Photographers
419 Park Ave. S., #1407
New York, NY 10016

American Women in Radio and Television
1101 Connecticut Ave., NW, Suite 700
Washington, DC 20036
(202) 429-5102
Susan Kudla Fuin, Exec. Officer

Asian American Journalists Association
1765 Sutter St., Suite 1000
San Francisco, CA 94115
(415) 346-2051
Diane Wong, Exec. Dir.

Association of Documentary Editing
c/o Celeste Walker
Massachusetts Historical Society
1154 Boylston St.
Boston, MA 02215
(617) 536-4042
Celeste Walker, Sec.

Association of Independent Music Publishers
P.O. Box 1561
Burbank, CA 91507

Association of Informational Media and Equipment
c/o Beverly Brink
P.O. Box 865
Elkander, IA 52043
(319) 245-1361
Beverly Brink, Exec. Sec.

Black Women in Publishing
P.O. Box 6275, FDR Station
New York, NY 10150
(212) 772-5951
Leslie Hunter, Pres.

Center for Communication
570 Lexington Ave., 21st fl.
New York, NY 10022
(212) 836-3050
Catherine Gay, Exec. Dir.

Freelance Network (Communications)
P.O. Box 36838 Miracle Mile Station
Los Angeles, CA 90036
(213) 655-4476
Michael Utvich, Pres.

International Association of Travel Journalists
P.O. Box D
Hurleyville, NY 12747
(914) 434-1529
Ron Bernthal, Dir.

Media Resource Service (Information Management)
355 Lexington Ave.
New York, NY 10017

Minorities in Media
P.O. Box 6538
Hampton Univ.
Hampton, VA 23668
(804) 851-8411
Dr. Samuel C. Still, Sr., Pres.

National Alliance of Third World Journalists
P.O. Box 43208
Columbia Heights
Washington, DC 20010

National Association of Black Journalists
P.O. Box 17212
Washington, DC 20041
(703) 648-1270
Carl E. Morris, Sr., Exec. Dir.

National Association of Broadcasters
1771 N St., NW
Washington, DC 20036
(202) 429-5300
Edward O. Fritts, CEO & Pres.

National Association of Hispanic Journalists
National Press Building, # 634
Washington, DC 20045

National Press Photographers Association
3200 Croasdaile Dr., Suite 306
Durham, NC 27705

Newspaper Systems Group
c/o James P. McCrystal
The Baltimore Sun
501 N. Calvert St.
Baltimore, MD 21278
(301) 332-6215
James P. McCrystal, Pres.

Speech Communications Association
  5105 Backlick Rd., Bldg. F
  Annandale, VA 22003
  (703) 750-0533
  James L. Gaudino, Exec. Dir.

Young Black Programmers Coalition (Broadcasters)
  P.O. Box 11243
  Jackson, MS 39213
  (601) 634-5775
  Robert Rosenthal, Mgr.

Recreational and Special-Interest Organizations

Cause-Related Organizations

Center for Responsive Governance
  1000 16th St., NW, Suite 500
  Washington, DC 20036
  (202) 223-2400
  Nelson M. Rosenbaum, Pres.

Media Coalition/Americans for Constitutional Freedom
  900 Third Ave., Suite 1600
  New York, NY 10022
  (212) 891-2070
  Christopher M. Finan, Exec. Dir.

Nuclear Free America
  325 E. 25th St.
  Baltimore, MD 21218
  (301) 235-3575
  Charles Johnson, Exec. Dir.

Peace Corps Partnership Program
  1990 K St., NW
  Washington, DC 20526
  (202) 606-3406
  Martha A. Holleman, Program Mgr.

Volunteers for Peace
43 Tiffany Rd.
Belmont, VT 05730
(802) 259-2759
Peter R. Coldwell, Exec. Dir.

Environment / Wildlife

American Alpine Club
113 E. 90th St.
New York, NY 10128
(212) 722-1628
Patricia A. Fletcher, Libn.

Center for Marine Conservation
1725 DeSales St., NW, Suite 500
Washington, DC 20036
(202) 429-5609
Roger E. McManus, Exec. Dir.

Citizens for a Better Environment
33 E. Congress, Suite 523
Chicago, IL 60605
(312) 939-1530
Jo Patten, Adm. Dir.

The Coastal Society
5410 Grosvenor Ln., Suite 110
Bethesda, MD 20814
(301) 897-8616
Dr. William Queen, Pres.

Environmental Action Coalition
625 Broadway, 2nd fl.
New York, NY 10012
(212) 677-1601
Nancy A. Wolf, Exec. Dir.

Geological Society of America
P.O. Box 9140
3000 Penrose Pl.
Boulder, CO 80301
(303) 447-2020
F. Michael Wahl, Exec. Dir.

National Geographic Society
  17th and M Sts., NW
  Washington, DC 20036
  (202) 857-7000
  Gilbert M. Grosvenor, Pres.

Outward Bound
  384 Field Point Rd.
  Greenwich, CT 06830
  (203) 661-0797
  John F. Raynolds III, Pres.

Rollin' Rock Club (Mineralogy)
  341 Senate Club
  Frankfort, KY 40601

Sierra Club
  730 Polk St.
  San Francisco, CA 94109
  (415) 776-2211
  Michael Fischer, Exec. Dir.

Minority / Special Interest Organizations

HEATH (Disabled)
  One Dupont Circle, Suite 800
  Washington, DC 20036
  (202) 939-9320
  Rhona Hartman, Dir.

Universal Negro Improvement Association and African Communities
  League of the World (UNIA & ACLW)
  5131 S. Wabash Ave.
  Chicago, IL 60615
  (312) 538-1349
  Charles L. James, Pres. Gen. & Admin.

On How to Write

Good writers develop; they are not born. Practice is at the heart of good writing. Both Gary and Carol have spent years writing, rewriting, and becoming comfortable talking on paper. If you are not used to writing, take some time to think about and act on the following tips. Not surprisingly, being a good writer is very similar to being a good speaker. You have to follow the same steps:

1. Evaluate other people's writing
   When you read the newspaper, magazines, or books, think about the author's purpose. Does the writing have impact? Does it move you, inspire you, anger or annoy you? What do you think the author is trying to accomplish? Could he or she write more effectively? How?

   If you think about and analyze other people's writing, you can become a better judge of your own work. Being able objectively to assess your own writing—to stand back and think how to improve what you've done—is central to refining and perfecting each project you write up.
2. Keep a journal
   In addition to recording your thoughts, a journal forces you to write every day. After a while, your thoughts become clearer and it becomes easier to express yourself. Being open and honest with yourself will help you be decisive in your writing. Try it.
3. Write letters
   In this age of advanced communication, good old-fashioned letter writing—even if it's on the word processor—is a good

discipline. Write your mom, your grandpa, your friends. Tell them what you've been doing. Tell them what you'd like to do. Ask them what they've been doing. You'll save money on your phone bill and you'll become a better writer.

4. Consider your reason for writing

   Writing a business letter is far different from sitting down to write your first novel. You have to know the purpose of your letter before you can begin to put your thoughts in order. What else do you need to know? Know what you want to accomplish. Do you want to persuade, inform, or compare and contrast a subject to make a point? Think about it.

5. Understand your audience

   Once you know your purpose for writing, you can start to think about who your audience is and the best means of reaching them. Are they young? Are they old? Are they cynical? Optimistic? Angry? Enthusiastic? Neutral? Open-minded? If you can connect with your audience at the outset, your writing will be much more pertinent.

6. Understand the writing process

   The writing process. I never understood what that meant until I read *The Simon & Schuster Handbook for Writers* (Prentice Hall, 1991). The author, Lynn Troyka, encourages writers to accept that good writing means clear thinking. Since few people or writers are good at thinking on their feet, it's best to allow time for your thoughts to develop and become refined over time. (This book is an excellent reference. Use it with a dictionary and keep both on your desk for easy reference.)

   How do you brainstorm? Write down everything you could possibly think of, once you select your topic.

   For example, say you want to write a paper on why your company should invest in videotapes as a means of sales training. You would start by brainstorming—that is, thinking of all the points which you want to make.

So let's do it.

Brainstorm list:
    Videos are a good learning method
    Videos are a fun, interesting medium

Sales training doesn't have to be boring
Role models should be used in sales training
Sales reps should be motivated by training

That's just a general list of ideas and points to make. Next, order those points—and think of any others—so that you can begin to write.

(In the work environment, you'll have to learn to think quickly.)

Back to the memo.

BUSINESS MEMO

1/7/93

To: National Sales Manager
From: Stephen S. Sales
Re: Opportunity for Video Training

On my recent field trip, I spoke to several of our reps, who suggested that we do video training on some of our key products. Here are the advantages:

1. In ten to twelve minutes you can teach a rep what he needs to know, without issuing reams of paper—our traditional sales method.
2. In addition to training our reps, we can use the same videos with our customers in committee presentations.
3. We can use the video as an image promotion when we try to sign new authors to work with us.
4. This is an opportunity to give our representatives a morale boost at a critical time of the year. We are not always able to act on their suggestions. Listening to them at this time would make an important statement.

Although we don't have money budgeted for this expense in this fiscal year, we should go ahead with the video because it will have an instant impact on sales. It will more than pay for itself. Plus, we'll have feedback from the reps on how to refine the idea for next season when we'll have plenty of time both to plan and budget.

Please let me know as soon as possible if I can proceed with the plans for the video.

Thank you.

Ideally, writers should write and revise their work two or three times. But in the real world of work, things happen quickly. You'll have to learn to process your thoughts rapidly so that you can respond within the given time period.

So, what type of writing are you most likely to do in your first few years on the job? You may write letters to customers, business prospects, associates, and others whom you meet.

Take a look at the sample letter.

BUSINESS LETTER

Kent Daniel
GraphicsAmerica
8194 Congress St.
Detroit, MI 60610
August 29, 199-

Ms. Margaret Garcia
XYZ Technology Company
55555 Wire Avenue
Silicon Valley, CA 18809

Dear Ms. Garcia:

GraphicsAmerica is pleased to introduce a new software line entitled Choice, a multi-purpose software program. Since your company uses a similar program with limited capacity, you are a perfect target for our product.

Enclosed please find the disks and software instructions. As a special incentive to try our product, we will send you a complimentary dictionary. All you have to do is view the software, print out an example from one of the options, and mail it back with the enclosed coupon. We hope this special incentive will encourage you to take the ten minutes required to look at this program and compare it to what you are currently using.

Please contact me collect if you have any questions: (415) 990-8873. Your business is important to me and I am committed to working with you on this and future projects.

Thank you for your time and consideration.

Sincerely,

Kent Daniel
Sales Representative

Encl.
cc: Myron Ranstein

MONTHLY REPORT

2/14/93

To: Lisa Brummel
cc: Ron Acker
From: Conrad Capp

Accomplishments:

Sales vs. Goal $189,000 actual / $175,000 goal

For the second month in a row, my territory is running ahead of our goal. To maintain this advantage, I have done the following in the last month:

1. Sent out a special mailing to all clients not currently using our product. I will track the response rate over the next month.
2. Met with all customers who adopted our product last year, to insure satisfaction and verify repeat orders. I also informed them of this year's product line, so that they could add to current orders.

3. Set up dates for next month's presentations. So far, I have scheduled five of my six targeted meetings.

Goals for next month:

1. Close business three weeks earlier than last year and bring it up at least four sales per day with a target of twenty per week.
2. Set up customer-focus group and get eighteen clients (minimum) to attend.
3. Set company goal for customer satisfaction by implementing the WE CARE ABOUT YOU service and follow-up program.

Expenses to date: $3,891

These are a few samples of writing which you are likely to do on the job. If you practice writing every day outside of work, you will be well polished when you are called on to write those last-minute, all-important reports.

On Speaking in Public

If you are not comfortable speaking in public—to small groups, to large groups, or to two or three people at a time, you may want to consider taking a public-speaking class at a local school or through an organized program like Dale Carnegie. There are also organizations—like the National Toastmasters Society—which provide monthly opportunities to give talks in front of others.

What is the benefit of a class?

Carol took a class at a local school a few years ago. The greatest advantage is being able to practice speaking in front of people you barely know. The teacher videotaped several of the sessions and the class critiqued each one. You can see your odd mannerisms, notice the pace at which you speak, and be more aware of what is and is not appealing.

The other benefit is that you get to think about other people—what they say and how they deliver their message—which of course makes you better at judging yourself.

What are some tips if you can't take a class?

You don't have to take a class to become a good speaker, although it helps. Here are some ways to help yourself:

1. Know why you have to speak. Are you speaking to persuade, inform, motivate, indict? You have to know what your purpose is and then work from there to figure out what to say and how to say it effectively.
2. Understand your audience. Read Dale Carnegie's book *How to Win Friends and Influence People*. This book has everything to do with effective speaking. Why? Because the premise of the book is: Understand your audience. If you don't know who you are

speaking to or what it is your audience is interested in hearing, you will have a more difficult time connecting with them.

3. Read some good speeches. You can find them in the newspapers—especially around election time—and you can turn on the TV and watch people speaking at press conferences, media forums, and other occasions. What is good or bad about what they do? What would you do better?

   One of our favorite speeches is Martin Luther King, Jr.'s "I Have A Dream" speech. Though few of us will ever have the vision or the forum for such a moving, important speech, we can learn a lot from King's style.

4. Practice. You can practice reading all kinds of things which will help you to become good at speaking in public. Read magazine articles aloud. Read poems, short stories, and toasts. If you are preparing for a speech, read it aloud several times and then read it in front of a mirror. How do you look? Are you comfortable? Are you confident? Do you look as if you are at ease with the material?

5. Use props. Whether you write your notes on index cards, use slides, transparencies, or a flip chart, you will probably need something, however brief or long, to keep your presentation focused.

6. Avoid reading your speech. This is tough to do and may take you a while. But the best speakers can look at their notes and appear to be speaking extemporaneously. They sound more compelling.

7. Vary your tone. Have you ever heard people speak who just drone on in the same tone of voice? Have you ever stayed awake for more than fifteen minutes when you've been subjected to these kinds of talks? Inject some emotion into what you say. You can raise and lower your voice when you want to make different points. You can enunciate clearly and speak out so you keep people's attention. Let them know you are not only alive; you are full of life and you have something to say.

8. Look around the room. Again, this is a more subtle point, mastered by the best speakers. If you can look out—not down or up or sideways—you are more likely to engage your audience. They want to feel as though you are having a conversation with them and they will if you make a point of looking in their direction once in a while.

Like good writing, good speeches take time. Plan what you want to say, think about it for a while, and then do a final draft. After you have written the speech, you can start practicing. Writing things out always helps to crystallize one's thoughts.

On being interesting

For most of the speaking you'll be doing in your first few years on the job, you'll need to know how to speak effectively to smaller groups of people. This involves more impromptu speaking in meetings and in person. Whether you are speaking to groups large or small, you want to be interesting. Here's how you can be interesting and get your point across:

1. Use examples

   Make specific references rather than generalizations. It is more interesting to say: "The widget, which was developed by hand in a Swedish workshop, has a great impact on the way we create, sell, and market fine cabinetry in the United States" than: "Widgets have done well in the United States."

2. Use analogies

   Good speakers often illustrate by analogy. Ed Stanford, Prentice Hall's president, gave a very effective speech at last year's sales conference. He compared the spring sales season to training for and running a race or marathon. The lessons were the same: Set reasonable but ambitious goals; get help; set benchmarks; maintain your stamina so you can endure the distance; enjoy the race.

3. Use quotes

   If well-known or sometimes not-so-well-known people have said something specific, dramatic, or pertinent to your subject matter, their words can give weight to your point. "Neither a borrower nor a lender be," the famous words from Shakespeare, may be a suitable introduction to a speech on the savings-and-loan crisis in America.

4. Use humor

   Gary had to give a speech recently on behalf of a team of people to a group of 250. He had only thirty minutes in which to describe the goals, purpose, and unique personality of his team. Gary's idea was to use the Addams Family as a unifying theme for the discussion.

   The result? The speech was very well received. The group

rented a video and played the introduction to the movie; each team member dressed up in Addams family outfits and so dressed gave his or her particular talk about the team and its members. The crowd loved it.

5. Tell stories

People often begin a speech with a story. Religious leaders do this all the time. I personally think that there is nothing more interesting than the wisdom of the oral tradition—that kernel which captures the essence of an experience. Carol has included this kind of story in the speech that appears on the following pages.

How do you learn to speak articulately at work?

Speak in public off the job. There are hundreds of ways you can do this. Carol's sister-in-law Julie is a reader at church. Every other Sunday, she gets up in front of the entire congregation and reads a lesson. She practices beforehand, but since she has now read for more than three years, it has become natural and fun for her.

Another friend of ours reads to a group of seven to eight elderly people each week. After a few months, he has become much more confident on the job because of his volunteer activities.

There are loads of opportunities. Look for them.

PUBLIC-SPEAKING SELF-ASSESSMENT

I am afraid to speak in public because:

At work I speak in public to:
Small groups   Medium-sized groups

Large groups

I plan to improve my public-speaking abilities in my spare time by:

I plan to improve my public speaking on the job by:

PUBLIC-SPEAKING CHECKLIST

_____ Think of a topic

_____ Understand/analyze the audience
Who are they?
What do they want to hear?
Why am I speaking to them?

_____ Write outline

What are the main points I want to make?

What is the best way to organize those points?

_____ Analyze outline
Do the topics flow properly?
Could the material be more interesting?

_____ Come up with examples and supporting points
Are the examples interesting?
Do they relate to the audience?

_____ Develop an appropriate anecdote or story
What will really illustrate your point to your audience?

_____ Rehearse by yourself

_____ Rehearse in front of anyone who will listen

_____ Rate yourself

What do you think? Is it good enough? Even if the answer is yes, keep practicing.

On the following pages you'll find a speech that Carol wrote for an audience of graduating college seniors a few years ago. Try to analyze the speech in terms of the checklist. There were seniors, graduates, parents, and professors in the audience.

Good evening.

It is a pleasure to be here tonight. I welcome any opportunity to come to Tucson to visit family and friends, but it was a special honor to be asked to speak to this talented group of people on this year's Evening of Excellence.

So, why am I here tonight? What advice do I have to give you about college and your career? Why am I qualified to talk to you?

Let me tell you a little story.

A few years ago, I found myself in Greece with one of my best friends. We had just spent a week in Athens soaking up ancient culture before heading off to the quiet island of Mykonos. If you have ever visited Greece or if you have ever seen pictures, you know that the blue-green of the Mediterranean juxtaposed with the bright white of the staggered houses is one of the most breathtaking, inspiring sights to behold.

It was on this island, looking out on the Mediterranean Sea from a beach chair, that I gained real perspective on myself and my life. Away from my answering machine, the voice-mail at work, the stack of papers in my in-box, the faxes received from across the miles, and my usual back-to-back schedule, there was time and space to breathe and think. Big picture, not just day-to-day.

What I discovered is that I was having a mid-twenties crisis. I liked my job as a marketing manager, but I had held the same job for three years. I didn't know what to do. Should I stay in marketing? Should I stay in publishing? Should I go back to school?

On top of these concerns, I had just broken up with my boyfriend. It dawned on me at last that I would have a lot of free time on my hands.

What really brought these thoughts to the surface was reading a book entitled *What Color Is Your Parachute?* by Richard Bolles. I recommend this book to people of all ages. More than any other book, it helped me to define my interests, my abilities, my strengths, and my short- and my long-term goals. It enabled me to analyze my values and it caused me to ask myself some tough questions about what I really wanted out of life.

So when there was nothing between me and the world except a big, expansive, gorgeous sea, all these things, which I wasn't even conscious of before vacation, seemed crystal-clear. And though some of these things were scary to confront, there was a comfort and an energy which came from being in a beautiful place and getting ten hours of sleep each night.

It was then and there that I realized how much people in college could benefit from asking themselves some of the same big-picture questions in the context of their own career choices. If college students could better understand themselves, then maybe more people would select their major and their career in accordance with their true aptitudes and interests. If they understood how to plan ahead and gather information on those fields that truly interested them, maybe more people could get jobs during their senior year and succeed once they graduated.

I had made up my mind. I was going to write *Majoring in the Rest of Your Life*.

So I went to buy a pad of paper at one of the stationery stores on the island, and I started to brainstorm what this book should contain. It should have tips on how to study, advice on how to balance school, work, and extracurricular activities; it should explain how to get internships and why they count so much with prospective employers; and it should also explain how to interview for a job, write a résumé, and research companies and graduate schools.

Since I had interviewed many college graduates who were applying for jobs with Prentice Hall, I knew exactly what did and didn't work in an interview. I had also become savvy at spotting experiences in their past—grades, leadership positions held, what types of jobs they had had, how they discussed their interests and abilities—which were indicators of how well they would do on the job.

And then, of course, the book would have to contain some of the advice my sage brothers had given me while I was in college. As the youngest in my family, I had no lack of advice—some practical, some absurd, some heeded, some ignored. But there was enough good in what they said—and enough encouragement in the advice—that it prompted me to do much more than I would have without their incessant needling.

I had taken their advice and worked a summer on Capitol Hill. I worked in New York the following summer for a non-profit organization, and the following semester I studied in Spain. Most important, I tried to gain as much as I could from my classes here at the University of Arizona. If I learned how to think deeply, how to analyze, how to solve problems, and how to write and express myself, then I would be able to learn any job once I graduated. But I understood that making a commitment to getting the best education I could was the most important thing I could do for my career and for my life.

Another bit of advice came from my companion on the trip:

"Interview recent graduates from different fields," Brenda said to me. "You should show college students through your interviews how different people are. They need to realize that no two people will approach things in the same way. This will give college students a sense of reassurance and an appreciation of their own unique abilities."

So I came home from Greece rested and tanned, with a pad of paper chock full of ideas for a book. Two weeks after that, I bought a computer, started writing in the evenings and on Saturdays. A year and a half later I had a finished manuscript.

That's why I'm here tonight.

Now what you're wondering is:

What advice can I give you in a speech which can only be twenty minutes long?

Well, if I could sum up the advice I have for college students, it would be the same as that which I have for working adults:

1. Learn all you can.
2. Balance your studies with extracurricular activities.
3. Find work you enjoy and dedicate yourself to it.

Learn all you can

That seems straightforward in college, but what does it mean once you graduate? It means keeping your mind active, alive, and sharp. Stretch yourself beyond what you're learning on the job. Start a book club, take a class, travel to a state you've never visited. Learning as much as you can after you graduate is just as important as learning while you're in college.

In some ways, it can be more important. When I took an art-history course at Columbia University a few years ago, I found I was much more focused on learning than I had been in school. Of course, concentrating on just one class is a lot easier than focusing on five or six. Beyond learning something new, I found it refreshing to be back in the classroom. I saw the world again through the eyes of a student.

Oddly enough, on the days following each class I returned to work feeling relaxed and recharged. I had more perspective on problems at work and more energy with which to solve them. My class became a great way to relieve stress; and I had a new arena in which my interests could develop.

Pursue extracurricular activities: volunteer

The second important balance in your adult life, and it will come as no surprise to this group, is volunteering. Whether you decide to give your time to the hospice, the homeless, the Big Brother, Big Sister program, or any other deserving cause, make sure that volunteering is part of your life's equation. You'll gain energy and strength when you need it most and you'll develop important qualities—such as patience, and the ability to motivate and comfort people—and skills—such as being able to organize events, manage people, and keep to a schedule.

When I taught English as a second language a few years ago, I volunteered with several other people who helped low-income students from Latin America to learn to speak English. What I discovered is that they helped me as much as I helped them. When I was at a low ebb, their stories of their families and their friends captured my imagination. And I developed patience and perspective as I watched people who worked hard all day—cleaning homes, operating elevators, and working in small shops and restaurants—eagerly struggle to conquer a new language and a new culture. Their courage was inspiring. Their challenges made my challenges seem very small.

I learned something else. Teaching is just like managing. You have to understand your students, because no two are alike and no two learn the same way. The art is in drawing the best out of each student, whatever their particular learning aptitude. Now that I have been a manager for three years, I realize that the best teachers and managers—and parents, for that matter—use the same techniques: they ask good questions, they guide instead of direct, and they believe in the potential each person has to offer, in the face of failure and success. And they keep their tongue between their teeth when people decide not to follow their advice.

Find work you enjoy

My third piece of advice is to *find work you enjoy and dedicate yourself to it*. If getting a good education is the most important thing you can do in school, then finding a job you enjoy is the most important thing you can do once you graduate. Sometimes it takes people a long time to find their niche.

I have been very fortunate. When I had my career crisis a few years ago, I came back from Greece with a clear perspective on who I was and what I wanted. After analyzing my situation, I discovered that I liked what I was doing—my job did play to my strengths—but I needed a new challenge. I wanted to stay in marketing, but I wanted to start managing people. I spoke to my boss and made my goals known. Two months later I was supervising two people, and a year and a half later I became manager of the department.

I am an anomaly. I have been with the same company since I graduated, because Prentice Hall has kept me challenged and motivated.

Many of my friends have had different experiences. After a few years working, one friend felt stifled by her job with a consumer products company. She went to business school and now works for Kraft. Another friend changed fields completely—from accounting to journalism. Another went to law school, practiced for three years, and then discovered that law really wasn't for her.

The point is:

Don't be afraid to change your job or your industry if you aren't happy with what you are doing after a few years. The same goes for a major you dislike if you are still an undergraduate.

Think about your interests and abilities, be honest with yourself about your strengths and weaknesses, and think about your short- and long-term goals.

You may decide after five or six years that you'd like to get your Master's. You may decide you'd like to be in a different field altogether. Maybe you'll take some time off and write a book. Whatever you decide, don't be afraid of change—whether it is confronting the boss for a promotion or handing in your resignation to pursue the job of your dreams.

My final thoughts this evening have very little to do with career advice and everything to do with maintaining your friendships and upholding the values of the honoraries. And though this has significance for all undergraduates, it is most immediate for the graduating members of the Mortar Board and Bobcats.

What I can tell you seven years after graduating is that I am very close to many people with whom I worked in the honoraries here at the university. One friend moved to New York two years after I did and became my roommate; one trained and ran the NYC marathon with me (she has since finished three Los Angeles marathons and I've retired), and another volunteers with a group of university alums once a month at a soup kitchen on New York's Upper West Side.

Several people from my Mortar Board group have come back to New York to visit, and others I have been fortunate enough to see on my travels for Prentice Hall. Collectively, we cover almost every industry and profession from a Ph.D. student in biology at Oxford to a chemical engineer with Procter & Gamble.

If that enthusiastic, diverse group were here this evening, I think we would join your parents and teachers in saying collectively:

We expect a lot from you.

We should. You are bright, talented, and you've had the benefit of a fine education. Now it's your turn to join the "real world" where there is no Evening of Excellence each spring. You'll have to keep your own score card of accomplishments and contributions. However far-flung your groups become, I hope you will remain close-knit and remember the values and the actions which brought you together here at the University of Arizona.

So, go forth. Make the most of your own potential and take every opportunity to seek and develop the best in those around you. And don't forget to take a vacation each year.

Good night. And good luck.

Handling Travel:

Keeping the Balance and Bagging

the Benefits

Many jobs include some form of travel. And if you don't start out traveling, chances are you will travel at some point in your career. If you are in a position where frequent travel is required, there are a number of things you can do to make the travel more comfortable and entertaining and less stressful and expensive.

The number-one key? Exert control over your travel, instead of letting your travel control you. It's easy to let bad food or noisy hotel rooms and expense accounts knock you out of your personal routine. But travel can also have a severe impact on your finances.

Travel: The personal side

Getting there

▶ *Planning your itinerary*

In all likelihood, when and where you travel will be determined initially by your manager or by the nature of your job, your territory, or your region. Still, you'll probably have some latitude in scheduling your arrival and departure times, where you stay, and what you do.

TRANSPORTATION TIPS

1. *Pad your time.* If your trip starts Monday, leave Sunday, say between 4 p.m. and five. This will give you time to check into your hotel, organize what you have to do for the following day and week, and settle in. Likewise, leave early or stay Friday night and relax. There's nothing worse than arriving home very late after a long trip when you have to spend the whole next day unpacking, doing laundry, and following up on the week's activities.

2. *Drive if you can.* Rent a car if you can. If your final or interim destination is less than two or three hours, you should drive your own car or rent a car, unless you work for a profligate company. It costs less, is less stressful than the airport, and you won't be stuck at your hotel relying on the people you have appointments with or on cabs for transportation.

3. *Cluster your travel.* If possible, cover long distances early in your trip. It's better to make one long flight and then several short flights than several medium long-distance flights. The same is true with driving. This avoids the risk of getting severely delayed or overly exhausted.

Your travel checklist

If you are a frequent traveler, it's a good idea to develop a packing checklist detailing all things you'll need during your trip. Without it, you'll forget something and be forced to replace it on your trip. Gary was the worst offender. For some reason, he had a mental block about shaving cream—he forgot it on every trip. It took no less than seven cans of it clogging his bathroom cupboard to convince him to make out an ongoing travel list.

Getting the goodies: incentive programs

Incentive programs are the single best benefit of travel. Most major travel-service companies have some kind of frequent-use program. Sign up and try to use one or two vendors whenever it makes sense for your timetable and finances. Carol and Gary have earned over fifteen free airline tickets in the last three or four years. A friend of theirs recently earned two tickets to Thailand.

Frequent-flyer programs are the most visible and easiest to join. Just sign up at any airline counter. Many hotel chains also offer free stays or prizes for accumulated travel in dollars spent. There are several guidebooks, and even some newsletters you can consult if you need more detailed information on frequent-travel incentive programs.

TIPS FOR MAXIMIZING YOUR INCENTIVE PROGRAM

1. *Sign up early and focus on one or two carriers/hotels.* As you travel more and more, you'll accumulate higher and higher credits. Continental, for example, offers three levels of achievement, and the payouts rise as you travel more. Simply put, you get more and more bonuses for less travel.

2. *Combine air, car rental, hotel, and credit cards.* All major airline programs offer additional points for their partners, which usually include car rental. These partnerships are easy to forget about. Make a point of checking into the partnerships at hotel checkout time.

Some carriers also offer Master and Visa cards that pay a point for every dollar charged. If you travel frequently, get reimbursed by your company; you can score thousands of miles by garnering a carrier credit card.

Handling your expenses

Expenses are handled differently by almost every organization. You should familiarize yourself with your organization's policies early on, so you don't spend money on things which aren't reimbursable. Also, it's easy for your personal finances to get out of whack if your company has strict guidelines about expense submission.

TIPS FOR HANDLING EXPENSES

1. *Document everything daily.* It's easy to lose track of miscellaneous expenses and cash expenditures. We strongly advise that you keep a daily running log and a separate envelope for all your receipts. Everyone hates "doing their expenses"; good record keeping makes it easier.

2. *Pace yourself financially.* You'd be amazed at how quickly your travel and expenses budget is used up. Spend slowly and wisely, so you have money for the long haul.

Combine professional and personal travel

Occasionally, you may find yourself traveling to a locale you'd like to spend some time in. If your schedule, finances, and organization permit it, tack some personal time on to your business trip. It'll save you, and in many cases your company, airfare. If your work and vacation destinations are in close proximity (say, San Francisco and Portland, Oregon), it's worth investigating layovers at your play destination. Shorter flights or a larger airport may offer savings.

Getting out

Being in an unfamiliar locale can be frustrating if you don't make plans ahead of time. If you are staying a few days, consider looking at a guidebook to the area (or contact the local chamber of commerce, or the AAA) to get ideas about what to do and see. Even if you are staying only one night, try to get out of your room. You can always talk to the people at the hotel's front desk. They can tell you where it's safe to go jogging, if there are restaurants and shops nearby, and even where you can see a movie.

Where to stay

After transportation, where you stay has the most to do with how well you'll feel when the trip is over. Financial and geographical constraints will probably determine where you stay. Most of the time, the trick is making the best hand out of the cards you've been dealt. Here are some ways you can make your stay more comfortable:

1. Locale is key. If possible, avoid airport hotels. Opt for less expensive, more luxurious properties close to your place of work. The cab fare is worth the extra sleep in the morning, and most airport hotels are overpriced and far away from decent food and any form of recreation.
2. Make your hotel your home—the little things you do make a difference. As much as possible, take advantage of hotel amenities to maintain your personal routine. If you work out, ask for a hotel with an exercise room and allow time in your schedule

to use it. If you like to relax, pack your bubble bath and a candle. (That's Carol's suggestion, not Gary's.)

3. Go out and *play!*

   While on the road, there is a huge temptation to spend your time in your room, working or watching TV. Without a car, getting around can be a hassle and travel drains you. But just as staying in bed all day seems to make you more tired, staying in the hotel for breakfast and dinner will take a deadly toll. At the very least, leave for dinner, a walk, or a movie. After all, when you're home, you don't stay inside all day. What's the point of travel if you don't venture forth to explore?

The quick tips

Transportation

▶ Cars

If you travel a lot by car, join AAA. If you have any car trouble, you can call at once for help. If you can afford it, you may also want to consider installing a car phone or a CB. You need to be able to communicate with people, especially as you travel long distances.

Stock your car trunk so that it can become your office away from home. If you carry extra envelopes, a stapler, stamps, and anything else you need on a regular basis, you'll be all set.

▶ Airlines

Sit up front. You're the last one on and the first one off.

Check only the baggage you can't carry. If you can carry all your luggage, you'll save time on every flight.

Don't eat airline meals unless you will otherwise miss a meal. It sounds stupid, but airline meals aren't real—they're never enough and you'll end up hungry later. (If you want to have a healthy snack, ask for the vegetarian meal.)

Work on the plane. It's dead time which you can use to follow up on the work of the day.

▸ *Hotels*

If you're fit, request the top floor. No one will be pacing the floors above you. Also, make sure you're nowhere near the elevator, the boiler room, or the ice machine. These areas are noisy twenty-four hours a day. Hotels, for the most part, serve good breakfasts and bad dinners. Ordering breakfast ahead can save you time.

Bring your own travel alarm.

Don't count on the low-budget hotels to have irons.

▸ *Have a plan: juggling*

If your daily work routine doesn't involve travel, then your work trip really means you are creating twice as much work for yourself because what you otherwise do normally doesn't stop when you travel. For this reason, it is important to make travel as self-contained as possible. Try not to bring home a lot of follow-up work that will cut into your normal work effort.

Business travel can be exciting and interesting. Keep yourself focused and organized and plan time to have fun. If you don't let the travel wear you down, you're likely to benefit from the experience.

Books for Further Reading

Leadership / Success

Seven Habits of Highly Successful People, Stephen R. Covey. Fireside, Simon & Schuster, 1989. Best-selling book that analyzes the common characteristics of successful people. Full of examples, it's quite invaluable.

On Becoming a Leader, Warren Bennis. Addison-Wesley, 1989. One of the classic books on developing leadership skills.

The Ten Dumbest Mistakes Smart People Make and How to Avoid Them, Dr. Arthur Freeman and Rose DeWolf. HarperCollins, 1992.

Lighten Up: Survival Skills for People Under Pressure, C. W. Metcalf and Roma Felibe. Addison-Wesley, 1992. How to use humor to control stress.

Future Trends / General Business Advice

Managing for the Future, Peter F. Drucker. E. P. Dutton, 1992. The well-known and highly respected management author writes clearly and persuasively about the challenges of the future.

In Search of Excellence, Thomas S. Peters and Robert H. Waterman. Warner Books, 1988.

A Passion for Excellence, Thomas S. Peters and Nancy K. Austin. Random House, 1985.

Thriving on Chaos, Thomas S. Peters. HarperCollins, 1988. Three classic business books that examine trends and make recommendations based on the activities of well-known organizations.

What They Don't Teach You at Harvard Business School, Mark H. McCormack. Bantam, 1986. Practical advice on topics from negotiation to organization from a leading sports and entertainment agent.

Workplace 2000: The Revolution Reshaping American Business, Joseph H. Boyett and Henry P. Conn. New American Library, 1991. Good fact-based discussion of the trends in business. Special emphasis on the new organization, international issues, and the environment.

What's Ethical in Business? Verne E. Henderson. McGraw-Hill, 1992. A discussion of the ethical issues facing business people, which uses numerous case studies.

Communication Skills

Winning Office Politics, Andrew Dubrin. Prentice Hall, 1990. Gives innumerable examples of strategies for handling tough situations and politics at work.

Working with Difficult People, Muriel Solomon. Prentice Hall, 1990. Examines several categories of difficult people and presents strategies for working with them.

Getting to Yes: Negotiating Agreement Without Giving In, Roger Fisher and William Ury. Viking Penguin, 1991. A classic book on negotiating.

Strategic Communication: The Art of Making Your Ideas Their Ideas, Burton Kaplan. HarperCollins, 1991. Good overview of written, verbal, and non-verbal communication.

The Business Presentations Workbook, Clark Lambert. Prentice Hall, 1988. Step-by-step workbook with which to put together business presentations.

Creativity

Creating, Robert Fritz. Fawcett Columbine, 1991. Largely theoretical discussion of how to build creativity at work.

The Creative Edge: How to Foster Innovation Where You Work, William C. Miller. Addison-Wesley, 1987. How to "cause" creativity at work, with an emphasis on making those around you more creative.

Thinkertoys, Michael Michalko. Ten Speed Press, 1991. Exercise-based workbook for building creativity.

Organizational Skills / Time Management

Time Power, Charles Hobbs. HarperCollins, 1987. This book presents a reasonable approach to organizing your life.

Five Days to an Organized Life, Lucy H. Hendrick. Dell, 1990. Down-to-earth advice on how to plan the details of your work and personal life.

How to Organize Your Work and Your Life, Robert Moskowitz. Doubleday, 1981. Classic book on setting priorities.

Career Opportunities

America's Fastest-Growing Employers: The Complete Guide to Finding Jobs with over 700 of America's Hottest Companies, Carter Smith. Bob Adams, 1992. Where the jobs are now, organized by company.

Peterson's Job Opportunities for Engineering, Science and Computer Graduates, Peterson's Guides, yearly editions. Aimed at the new college graduate, provides detailed company profiles of hundreds of potential employers.

Peterson's Job Opportunities for Business and Liberal Arts Graduates, Peterson's Guides, yearly editions. Same as above, for the non-technical among us.

Jobs 92: Leads on more than 40 million jobs and how to get them, Kathryn and Ross Petras. Prentice Hall, 1992. Provides information on growth areas by region of the U.S.

The American Almanac of Jobs and Salaries, John W. Wright and Edward J. Dwyer. Avon, 1990. Gives an overview of wages and jobs for all major occupations in the U.S. A good way to see if your salary is at a standard level.

The 100 Best Jobs for the 90's and Beyond, Carol Kleiman. Dearborn Financial Publishing, 1992. Focuses on specific business growth areas, but takes into account the overall work environment.

Everybody's Business: A Field Guide to the Four Hundred Leading Companies in America, Milton Moscowitz. Doubleday, 1990. Evaluates companies according to size rather than growth or work environment.

Jobs in Paradise, Jeffrey Maltzman. HarperCollins, 1990. How to get jobs in unusual locales when the location is more important than the job itself.

Moonlighting: 148 Great Ways to Make Money on the Side, Carl Hausman and the Philip Lief Group. Avon Books, 1989. Interesting ideas for expanding your income.

Career Advice / Changes

The 1992 What Color Is Your Parachute, Richard Nelson Bolles. Ten Speed Press, 1992. The all-time classic book for making career decisions.

Do What You Love, the Money Will Follow, Marsha Sinetar. Dell, 1989. Interesting best-seller that provides the steps for pursuing what you love and turning it into income.

How to Market Your College Degree, Dorothy Rogers and Craig Bettinson. MGV Career Horizons, 1992. Finding a job for the college graduate.

Marketing Yourself, Dorothy Leeds. HarperCollins, 1991. No-holds-barred professional advice that emphasizes using real-world marketing techniques like direct mail to land a job.

Out of the Organization, Madeleine and Robert Swain. MasterMedia, 1992. Outlines new opportunities like freelancing, starting your own business, jobs not involving a typical organization.

Fired for Success, Judith A. Dubin and Melanie R. Keveles. Warner Books, 1990. For the recently laid-off or fired, this book takes you through the steps to securing your next job.

Guerrilla Tactics in the New Job Market, Tom Jackson. Bantam, 1991. Aggressive advice for a competitive job market. Non-traditional, but full of a lot of unusual tips.

Star Teams, Key Players: Successful Career Strategies for Women in the 90's, Michele Jackson and Susan Waggoner. Henry Holt, 1991. Looks at the role of women in business and discusses how to take advantage of the changing workplace.

Guides to Managing Your Finances

Wealth Without Risk, Charles J. Givens. Simon & Schuster, 1991. Classic book on building wealth.

Marshall Loeb's 1992 Money Guide, Marshall Loeb. Little, Brown, 1992. The editor-in-chief of *Fortune* offers strong advice on investing and managing more complicated financial matters.

Making the Most of Your Money, Jane Byrant Quinn. Simon & Schuster,

1991. Adapted from her popular weekly column in *Newsweek*, this book is practical, but runs the gamut of financial matters.

Smart Money: How to Be Your Own Financial Planner, Ken Dolan and Daria Dolan. Wiley, 1987. Down-to-earth but professional financial-planning guidelines.

DO YOU HAVE ADVICE?

If you have advice or a story of your own to contribute for the next edition of this book, we would love to hear from you. Take a few moments to write below what you did and didn't like about this book—we would really appreciate it.

	Yes	No
1. This book gave me a realistic understanding of what was expected of me in the working world.	_____	_____
2. I liked the opinions which this book offers.	_____	_____
3. This book helped me to feel more comfortable about life after college.	_____	_____

4. I would improve this book by: (check one)

_____ Adding more examples

_____ Using fewer examples

_____ Other _____

5. I would recommend this book to my friends.   _____ _____

6. I found out about this book by: (check one)

_____ Seeing it in a bookstore.

_____ It was a gift.

_____ It was assigned in a class.

7. I would improve this book by:

Thank you for your suggestions. Please mail this form and any other comments to:

Carol Carter and Gary June
Graduating into the Nineties
Farrar, Straus and Giroux
19 Union Square West
New York, NY 10003

Your name and address: _____

_____

_____

Phone: _____

Do we have permission to quote you?   Yes_____ No_____
Do we have permission to contact you?   Yes_____ No_____